MODERN DRUMMER® Legends

Chad Smith

Subscribe to *Modern Drummer*: moderndrummer.com/subscribe

For fun and educational videos, subscribe to the
"Modern Drummer Official" YouTube channel

Modern Drummer Publisher/CEO **David Frangioni**

Managing Director/SVP **David Hakim**

Managing Editor **Michael Dawson**

Art Director; Layout and Design **Scott Bienstock**

Music Transcription **Terry Branam**

Front and back cover photos by Tony Woolliscroft

Published by:
Modern Drummer Publications, Inc.
315 Ridgedale Ave #478
East Hanover, NJ 07936

Contents

Tony Woolliscroft

Rhythmic Party Starter

"I have so much invested in this band, and I'm proud of it. It's part of my identity. That's not to say I couldn't do other things, but I live The Red Hot Chili Peppers."

When Chad Smith said these words to *Modern Drummer* in August of 1999, the drummer might have inadvertently nailed the secret to his band's success. To be sure, The Red Hot Chili Peppers are one of the biggest rock groups in history, by any measure. And like all legendary bands—from The Beatles, to Led Zeppelin, to U2—the power of The Chili Peppers lies in the unique chemistry of its members. There is no "I" in rock 'n' roll, and Chad Smith, as awesome a drummer as he is, knows this intimately.

Born and raised in the Detroit suburbs, Chad Smith took the well-worn rock route to stardom: garage bands, endless cover gigs, eventual major-label support…and subsequent disappointment. Chad knew that if he was going to take this rock thing seriously, a move to the city of promise, LA, was in order. So he packed his bags, entered music school there, and promptly met the guys with whom he would capture that elusive brass ring. Several decades, a million road miles, a novel's worth of personal drama,

and a bunch of record-breaking, trend-setting albums later, and The Red Hot Chili Peppers are a bona fide American institution. To an entire generation, their distinct blend of funk, rap, punk, and classic rock makes them the ultimate get-down party band, willing to put their blood, dignity, and lives on the line in the quest for a righteous groove.

Along the way, Chad's own groove has deepened and matured, to the point where he has been able to go into the studio with such un-Peppery acts as John Fogerty, Johnny Cash, and The Dixie Chicks, and, simply, do the right thing, elevating the music with his big ears and super-consistent and energetic support. But, ultimately, Chad Smith is a band guy, and with each new release receiving some of the best reviews of their career, there seems to be no immediate end to The Red Hot Chili Peppers' incredible run at the top of the charts, and in the hearts of music fans across the globe.

The compilation of this book includes all of Chad's cover stories for *Modern Drummer* over the years, plus a smattering of shorter pieces, a new exclusive interview, and a deep-dive style and analysis of Smith's greatest drum hits with the Chili Peppers and beyond.

A NOTE FROM THE PUBLISHER

Chad Smith has been inspiring drummers for decades through his prolific work with Red Hot Chili Peppers, Ozzy Osbourne, Joe Satriani and Chickenfoot. Chad is the quintessential drummer fusing rock and funk with a unique approach to whatever band he's driving. I have never seen Chad perform at a level any less than a "10," he brings THAT much energy and passion to every drum stroke. His Modern Drummer covers are some of the most creative and innovative covers we have ever produced. Chad was the brainchild behind every one of them.

As incredible of a drummer as Chad is, I've gotten to know him personally and am blown away by how kind, passionate and humble he is as a person. His charity work is seemingly endless working with various non-profit organizations and helping people in need. Chad Smith is a true drumming legend and we cannot wait for you experience what's in your hands right now, the world of Chad Smith Legends!

David Frangioni
CEO/Publisher of Modern Drummer Publications, Inc.

Conviction

The 2021 Interview

by Mark Griffith

The Red Hot Chili Peppers are one of the most influential bands in rock and roll. Period. And Chad Smith is the glue that holds it all together. He can go note for note with bassist Flea, or he can be the rock that grounds it all when the rest of the band is bouncing impressionistic rhythmic waves off of each other. His passion for all music is palpable and infectious, as are his grooves. Through his work with legendary producer Rick Rubin, Chad has also recorded with musical legends like Johnny Cash and The Chicks (formerly The Dixie Chicks.) Elsewhere Chad has recorded with Kid Rock, John Fogerty, Ozzy Osbourne, Chickenfoot, and The Avett Brothers. He also leads his own band called the Bombastic Meatbats. But you already know all of that. Afterall, Chad Smith is a *LEGEND*.

When Chad and I sat down, I was determined to ask him questions that he has never been asked before. Together we broke down how he creates beats within the Red Hot Chili Peppers' music, talked about some of his favorite bands and drummers, and talked about geography.

MD: You grew up in Detroit; can you offer your perspective on what is a Detroit drummer?

Chad: Obviously there is the Motown thing, and there is a strong jazz tradition too, but it's so much more than that. The people of Detroit are really special. There is unique grit there; the city of Detroit has developed a work ethic that is known around the world. The people of Detroit work hard, and when they're done working, they play hard, and they party hard. So when I was coming up playing six nights a week in bar bands on that scene (and there was a really strong scene there) it was really important to give everything you had when you were on stage. When people came to see the bands that I was in, I had to really bring it. In Detroit, you have to play with absolute conviction, because if you don't, people will see right through you, and they will leave, instantly.

There are some great Detroit drummers that never get talked about, guys like John Badnajek from Mitch Ryder and the Detroit Wheels. He also played with Edgar Winter, Alice Cooper, and Bob Seger. He is one of my favorite drummers *ever*! He also had a band called The Rockets. John wore these funny little sunglasses, and he would just keep his head down and wail. He had a gigantic groove. If you haven't checked him out, you have to!

There was also Jimmy Marino from the Romantics. People always think of Jimmy Marino singing "What I Like About You" on MTV. But he was so much more than that. He has a ferocious groove too. I used to hear him on the local Detroit scene all of the time.

Those two guys were a huge influence on my drumming, and (to me) their conviction personified Detroit drumming. They really meant it.

Tony Woolliscroft

MD: I know you're a sports fan, I recently found a great quote from New York Yankee pitcher David Cone regarding the word *conviction*. You can change all the baseball terms to musical or drumming terms and it conveys the same message: "If a pitcher isn't 100 percent sure he's throwing the right pitch, it doesn't matter if the finger pressure, the arm-slot, the stride-length, and follow-through are all perfect. Without that last piece—conviction—that pitch is going to get hit. I promise you."

Chad: I completely agree. And even if you aren't sure, you just have to…

they brought their own stuff with them. It's easy to say the California thing is laid back, and all that. But it's more than that; there is a well rounded-ness to a California drummer.

MD: I want to try and deconstruct your band's groove, and at the same time dissect your playing and your groove concept a bit. In past interviews, I have asked many of the funkiest drummers (Mike Clarke, David Garibaldi, Zigaboo Modeliste) this question. All of you play in bands with really busy or percussive bassists, and yet you never seem to get in each other's way. How does that work? Do you and Flea ever step on each other toes? Because I've never heard it happen, and

Tony Woolliscroft

MD: …fake it till you make it!

Chad: You got it.

MD: So conversely, you have now been in California for a long time, and people often refer to the Red Hot Chili Peppers as the quintessential California band. What is a California drummer?

Chad: Wow, I gotta think about that… Well, you know no one is *really* from California; almost everyone comes here from someplace else. Shelly Manne is from New York, Hal Blaine is from Massachusetts, Jim Keltner is from Oklahoma, and Earl Palmer is from New Orleans. When they all got here

it would seem impossible to think that it hasn't happened?

Chad: Yeah sure we have; it's going to happen. But if that happens, it just takes a look between us, and usually I will pull back a bit and just find less notes to play without destroying or abandoning the groove. I don't mean to play it "boring," because that shows lack of conviction as well. But just sometimes, you can leave a little bit more space. And that comes from really listening, that's what it all comes down to.

When we were all younger, we had a real tendency to fill up a lot more space. And maybe that's what you are supposed to do when you're a young musician. But as we have all matured, we have found the beauty of leaving a little more space. I'm starting to think that everyone has to evolve that way.

MD: What is your natural tendency, to play the bass drum with the bass parts, or to find the holes and fill in the blanks?

Chad: I am definitely a bass and bass drum locking-up guy. That's where I go to first. But if that doesn't work for that song, I'll find another approach and look for some holes.

MD: What is the difference in creating drum grooves with Flea and with Michael Anthony in Chickenfoot?

time, and hit it with me. So with him I'm probably listening more to the rest of the tune, because there is a lot going on in Chickenfoot with Joe Satriani and Sammy Hagar as well.

MD: How much do you listen to or relate to the rhythm guitar parts?

Chad: Well, that the drummers' best friend, you know that! Everyone always talks about the drum and bass thing, but the rhythm guitar part is really where it's at. Peppers' guitarist John Frusciante is a guitar player that I think would almost rather play rhythm guitar than solo. And I am always tuned into his rhythm playing. I keep the whole band in my

Tony Woolliscroft

Chad: Those two guys are very different players. As you said, Flea is very percussive and very rhythmic. Not that Mike isn't rhythmic, but Mike has that great rolling sixteenth-note thing. Everyone talks about his vocal contribution to Van Halen with his high vocals. But Mike's groove is powerful and just relentless.

MD: So when Mike gets those sixteenth notes going, how do you find your space?

Chad: Again I might just lay back a bit, and give him his space. He has great ears, so if I find an accent to play within his groove, or within the tune, he will be all over it the next

monitors, so I am listening to everything.

MD: Do you ever let the rhythm guitarists sound or approach dictate your hi-hat playing?

Chad: Not consciously, but now that you mention it, I probably do. I'll let his rhythm playing help me determine where some cool hi-hat barks might fit. Or maybe I'll let his sound determine how much I open the hi-hat. I've never really thought about it, and I'm definitely *not* thinking about that when we're playing. But yeah, subconsciously I think I do that.

MD: How do you let the lyrical content affect how you play a tune or a groove?

Chad: Hal Blaine used to always ask artists for the lyric sheets. He really wanted to know what a song was about. I do that too because it does help to know what the song is about. The problem is that sometimes Anthony Keidis [singer for the Red Hot Chili Peppers] is often a little vague regarding what a song is actually about.

MD: Let's go back to the fact that everyone in the Peppers is really rhythmical. Anthony is scatting a million miles an hour, Flea is doing his percussive bass thing, and John is such a great rhythm guitar player… So with all of that rhythmic space being occupied, you always seem to find your space, how do you do that?

Chad: Again, sometimes I just have to pull back, and play really simply, and let everyone else play.

MD: So in a way, you are acting as the bass player of the band, just laying it down and supporting everyone else doing their thing.

Chad: Yeah, I'm the Michael Anthony of the Red Hot Chili Peppers. I never thought of it that way. [laughs] But I do what Mike often did in Van Halen.

But you know what's cool? I just did a Morrissey record last week, and I was the last guy to add his parts. So I could really hear what was happening in the tune, and I created my drum parts in response to what everyone had already laid down on the tracks. That's a really different way of playing, and I like that too.

MD: Speaking of lyrics and singers, when I listen to the Ozzy record that you did, was I hearing some Bill Ward influenced stuff coming out?

Chad: I hope so, and really how could I *not* play like Bill when I am hearing *that* voice of Ozzy's coming through the headphones. Ozzy has one of the greatest and most unique instruments (his voice) in rock and roll. Before I did that record I went back and listened to some of the last few Ozzy solo records, and I just felt like that "swing" was missing behind Ozzy. So I really just wanted to bring some of that back to his music. Bill Ward was always one of my favorites, and no one really talks about him. His playing had such a strong swing to it. He really was a jazz drummer playing in one of the greatest metal bands ever. Then you had Geezer doing his thing, and Tony with the riffs. I love Sabbath!

MD: So here's a question that has probably never been asked of anyone. Does Ozzy Osbourne swing?

Chad: In his own way, yeah he's swingin'!

MD: I hear Sabbath in a similar way to the Red Hot Chili Peppers. Everyone has such a unique and distinct voice, and somehow it just found a blend and a created unique musical mix.

Chad: But back to Bill, what he did with Sabbath was so unique; he had a really loose time-feel. If I played anything that sounded remotely like him with Ozzy, I'll take that!

MD: All those guys had a strong swing feeling in their drumming.

Chad: I think I also played some Ian Paice sounding stuff

with Ozzy too. I love Deep Purple.

MD: In going back through your interviews, you have never been asked specifically about P-Funk, and I hear such a strong influence there, can you talk to me about your P-Funk influence? Who's your favorite P-Funk drummer?

Chad: Probably Tiki Fullwood. He played on all my favorite tunes. P-Funk is about repetition and, here's your word again, *conviction*. With P-Funk, it was all about the rhythm section controlling the dynamic of the entire band, because if they didn't, it could get really out of control. When you listen to P-Funk, you can hear the rhythm section shaping the entire tune. You know, when you have thirty musicians on stage, it can get really crazy, and (from what I've heard) George Clinton would get a little bugged. So in those times, the rhythm section had to take charge. In past interviews I've talked a little about playing with percussionist Larry Fratangelo in Detroit and what he taught me about P-Funk.

MD: He played percussion with P-Funk when Dennis Chambers was in the band, right?

Chad: Yup.

MD: But you never got specific. What did he teach you? What were the P-Funk lessons?

Chad: One big thing was when it was getting really loud, the drummer would hit a big crash on one and leave out the backbeat on two, that space would automatically bring the band down.

MD: I've heard a lot of the older blues drummers do that too.

Chad: Absolutely! P-Funk has great "band time." Which is different from "great time." They all feel the one in the same way. They all accelerate, and slow down at the same time. The whole band just breathes together. I think after thirty years or so, we have developed that sort of thing in the Chili Peppers.

I also learned about the beauty of the four-on-the-floor groove from listening to P-Funk, and how it is *so* different from playing bass drum on just 1 and 3. I always (incorrectly) thought, *Don't play on the 2 and 4 with the bass drum because that's where the snare drum belongs, let's not clutter things up.* Well, I was wrong! There is nothing as powerful as the four on the floor groove. It's such a different feel from playing the bass drum on 1 and 3 and the snare on 2 and 4, and P-Funk is all about that four-on-the-floor groove. They really show you the power of repetition in the groove. When I was

Tony Woolliscroft

younger I probably didn't want to learn about that, or I didn't want to listen when someone told me, but groove is really about repetition.

MD: Speaking of repetition, I know you have worked a lot with Rick Rubin. He produced one of my favorite records that is all about repetition: the *Live* record by the D.C. go-go band Trouble Funk. What has he brought to your playing and your groove?

Chad: Yeah Trouble Funk was baaad—talk about groove. Rick never really makes obvious suggestions or comparisons between the people that he has worked with…except for

Chad: I know. But Rick is just the biggest fan of music that there is. He just loves all music. So it's great to have him there, because he doesn't have any emotional attachment to anything in our tunes. He just knows when he likes it. Sometimes he'll just sit and listen. People don't know what he's "actually *doing*," but he's listening. He'll make little suggestions on how something could be different, but he rarely makes absolute musical recommendations.

MD: He has called you for a lot of sessions that he has done. Has he ever told you why he likes to bring you in?

Chad: Rick and I share a really deep passion for music.

one time.

MD: When was that?

Chad: We were playing a break, and Rick wanted this blast-beat Slayer-type of thing, and I played it—*or I tried to,*—and Rick just looked at me… I tried it a few more times, and he just didn't dig it. I wasn't really nailing it.

MD: Maybe it was lacking some of that Slayer conviction?

Chad: Probably! I knew it; I'm not the drummer from System of a Down either. So he sent me a System of a Down track, and told me to play it like that.

MD: Easier said than done.

He knows how I play, and he knows who and how I am. I'm going to bring in a good vibe. I'm not going to come in all miserable and bring everyone down. I bring a good personality to the situation. He knows that I'm *not* a "session drummer." I can't do everything. I think he brings me in when he feels like a band is looking for something, musically, that I can provide. That's what happened with the Dixie Chicks, and with Johnny Cash.

MD: Maybe he's just looking for some of that Detroit conviction.

Chad: Right on!

Impressions

June 1993

Chad Smith On...

by Ken Micallef

Ask this Red Hot Chili Pepper about his favorite drummer, and you won't get yarns about heavy metal heathens or the Funky Drummer, parts one, two, or three. Chad Smith is a student of music history, and his favorite drummer is none other than studio legend Hal Blaine. "Hal is the coolest guy I know," says Chad. "And he tells the best stories. He's so full of life. And he thinks the Chili Peppers are groovy."

Chad's groovy, thundering beat can be heard on the Chili Peppers' Mother's Milk and Blood Sugar Sex Magik albums. His solid tempo and a smart use of plentiful chops have brought Chad to the attention of millions of Chili Pepper fans and not a few drummers. Since the mid-'80s the Peppers have delivered a sound that combines greasy funk/metal/hipster slang/hip hop with all the politeness of an artillery cannon. Headlining last summer's Lollapalooza tour, the group appeared half-naked in diapers and bandannas (which didn't seem all that strange amidst a tour line-up that included glass eaters, bile drinkers, and one guy who stuck himself full of pins and needles). "We're a bowl of hardened Jello now," says Chad, regarding the result of months of touring. "On *Blood Sugar Sex Magik* we wanted to play for the songs, not just a lot of licks. After the touring we really love and respect each other; we know each other better now. We're maturing more as players and songwriters."

Who does Chad cite as influences? "The Marx Brothers, the 3 Stooges, and Robert DeNiro," he replies. "Life things more than just musicians."

...Steve Jordan

John Scofied: "Who's Who?" (from *Who's Who?*)
Chad: This kind of a Weather Report thing. Not quite as ethereal as them. The drummer was good. Cymbal sounds were really cool, nice textures and colors. His left hand was killing. Lots of chops. In that sort of vein, it's a good medium to stretch out in. No vocalist to step on, it's instrumentally oriented.
MD: It's Steve Jordan.
Chad: Oh, yeah. Back then he probably didn't have the double hi-hat thing going, right? He still got a lot of hi-hat into it. That was not bad. I wonder if he can still do all that?

...Stewart Copeland

Animal Logic: "Rose Colored Glasses" (from *Animal Logic II*)
Chad: That's Stewart Copeland. He's got that amazing hi-hat technique. On Peter Gabriel's "Red Rain," which is mostly drum machine, he just plays hi-hat, and it stands out. That's his signature. When the Police came out back in the '70s, everyone was into that wet, Eagles sound with the 9,000-foot snare drum. He brought a fresh, real tight thing. I sat behind him once in Detroit. He's the most powerful guy I've seen who plays traditional grip. His hands were all bandaged up, and he had that punk attitude—just slamming. It's nice that Copeland has done so much since the Police. He's written operas and soundtracks, done *The Rhythmatist*, and played in Animal Logic.

...Jeff Porcaro

Guitar Workshop: "Bawls" (from *Guitar Workshop In L.A.*)
Chad: With that shuffle/swing groove I can immediately tell it's Jeff Porcaro. He was the king of that stuff. Ever since "Rosanna" he's been known for that. When we were recording *Mother's Milk*, he was doing a session with Natalie Cole in the next room. We were both using Drum Doctors, the drum rental service. Jeff came in to say hi at about 10:00 in the morning. We were playing, and I didn't even know he was there. Afterwards he said to me, "Hey man, we've got to break your arms, or you'll be taking all my work!" I said, "Yeah, right!" He sat down to play a little bit and what did he do? Busted into a little shuffle, what else?

... Aaron Comess

Spin Doctors: "What Time Is It?" (from *Pocket Full Of Kryptonite*)
Chad: That sounds nice. Who is it?
MD: Aaron Comess with Spin Doctors.
Chad: Oh, yeah? He sounds good. He's a little slick for my taste, but he can play. Those are interesting triplet fills he's playing in the bridge, and his touch is nice. He sounds like he practices a lot. Strong chops. Good player—absolutely.

For newer drummers, I'm into Fish from Fishbone, the drummer from the Bad Brains, and Stephen Perkins of Jane's Addiction. Primus's drummer Tim "Herb" Alexander is happening, too. There are a lot of good players out there.

Ask a Pro
September 1994
Kick Drum Chops

After listening to the Chili Peppers' *Blood Sugar Sex Magik*, I felt that the drums were just incredible. I was especially impressed at how closely your bass drum chops complemented the bass lines. Can you suggest an exercise that would help me improve my bass-drum playing? You're a great inspiration for up-and-coming drummers.
Chris

Let me first say that you are obviously a man of impeccable taste! But seriously, with regard to your comments: The Peppers are a very rhythm-oriented band, and with our brand of funk, the bottom end (Flea and myself) propels the band with often-syncopated feels. Therefore, it's essential that we lock into each other's playing. Hands and feet are great, but don't forget about the ears!

Improving your kick drum work is a lot about balance. Try sitting down at your kit without your sticks. With your feet, alternate rudiments (like paradiddles or triplets) or try to get a smooth samba pattern going. It feels weird not to use your hands, but it's great for balance and independence. Oh, and don't leave the beater against the head. Hit the drum and get off it. It's less work and it sounds better, too.

Tony Woolliscroft

"We're an energetic bunch. When we play, it's full-throttle."

The December 1994 Interview

by Adam Budofsky

"I'm paying homage to the fathers of the drumset. We owe those guys a lot." Chad thought it would be cool to be photographed in a similar look and expression to some of drumming's early masters. You may recognize a bit of Gene Krupa. Buddy Rich, and even Dave Tough in a few of these photos. [Chad would like to thank Brian Irving and the Professional Drum Shop of Hollywood, California for the use of the vintage drums.]

"We're an energetic bunch. When we play, it's pretty much balls-out, full-throttle."

If you don't know at least that much about the Red Hot Chili Peppers...shame shame, you haven't been paying attention. Underground dance-floor faves, darlings of MTV and Top-40, tattooed trend-setters—the Peppers have fused funkadelia and punk abandon to create their own butt-shakin', head-bangin', super-energized sound.

When Chad Smith auditioned for the band in '88 to replace the exited Jack Irons (recently of the band 11), he recognized the energy at the core of that sound right away. "I didn't have any pre-conceived notions; I just went down and jammed. It was really fun. Everyone was laughing and yelling at each other. I was thinking, yeah, this is *good*."

Lots of people agreed. *Mother's Milk* came out in '89 and spread the word further and wider. In '91 it was *Blood Sugar Sex Magik*, the breakout album that spawned hit after hit: "Give It Away," "Under The Bridge," "Breaking The Girl." Then, Lollapalooza. The Grammys. Mass exposure. A slew of punk-funk imitators, most of whom can't touch the Peppers' power and ingenuity.

As the band's star began to rise, so did Chad's. More ads began appearing in music mags—Chad underwater in a giant aquarium, Chad smoking a cigar in an angel suit, Chad

Michael Bloom

chomping on a crash cymbal.... Not many drummers could get away with such silly antics, but the fact is, Smith's seriously solid and funky drumming—om album, live, and at clinic appearances—lent so much credibility to his reputation that no one seemed to care. A video on DCI and a corresponding book soon appeared, followed by a (not soon to be forgotten) spot at Modern Drummer's Festival Weekend '94....

Now it's mid-summer; by night the Chili Peppers are finishing up their as-yet-unnamed new album, by day they're rehearsing at SIR Studios in Hollywood for Woodstock '94 and a short European tour. As I walk down the corridor toward the rehearsal room, strains of "Give It Away" get progressively louder. I peak my head through the door and catch Chad's eye. He smiles from behind his Pearl "Octopus" kit and motions toward a leather couch where drum tech Louis Mathieu sits.

The band is ripping it up. No, there weren't any light-bulb heads in sight, and everybody was fairly clothed. But these guys were rockin' way harder than most bands do at actual shows—Flea is digging into his bass and unconsciously doing his patented head roll, singer Anthony Kiedis has his rap stance happening, newcomer Dave Navaro (late of Jane's Addiction) is testing his six-string pose on a monitor speaker. Chad, at the center of the tornado, is *slamming* away. From this scene, it's obvious that the live Chili Pepper energy comes from a very real and sincere place.

"I'm not *that* much of a showman," Chad half-convincingly says later, "but I am enjoying myself, and I think people can see that. I'd never let the theatrical stuff get in the way of the actual drumming, but when you're comfortable and playing what's in your heart and soul, people pick up on that sort of honesty. It's gotta be a natural thing, though, not like, 'You're crazy! You're zany! You're wacky! Okay, you're a Chili Pepper.' You just gotta be who you are. I think that's part of why they wanted me to join the band. With any good musician, part of the way they sound is their personality flowing out of their playing."

After rehearsal, Chad's Harley leads us to a classic old Hollywood restaurant, where we try to get to the root of that Chili Pepper energy.

Chad: For me, it's really about kicking those guys' asses. Of course, there are dynamics in the music, but I've always got to be really powerful, really solid. At the beginning of a tour, I might think about conserving energy, but I get so excited, I just get out there and start cranking. And if at the end of the show I'm dying, then I just won't party the next night.

MD: How about tempos? Does all the excitement and energy ever affect that?

Chad: Oh, don't think that when we were at Woodstock we weren't feeling like... [Chad air-drums and sings a double-time parody of "Give It Away."] It's a thing we all talk about. You've gotta relax. Flea is pretty good about tempos. Dave gets excited and always wants me to count shit off. For a

Michael Bloom

while some things used to be fast. I used to tape stuff just to see.

MD: What do you do to control tempo?

Chad: Usually I'll think, *Okay, here's where I'm feeling it, and then I'll try to just kick it back a little from there.* That compensates for the adrenaline factor. Then it's usually in the pocket and everyone's like, "Yeah." I try to give everything its full value, make it really fat without dragging. We have all these things going back and forth: "Kick back but make it really exciting! Put it in the pocket, but then you really gotta go!" And if it ends up feeling a little excited, that's okay.

MD: In your video...

Chad: You've seen my video?

MD: I have indeed seen your video.

Chad: So you know all this stuff.

MD: I even have your book in my bag.

Chad: Jesus Christ, don't embarrass me any more than I

already am.

MD: For those who don't have the video or book...

Chad: Go out and buy them cause I get like twenty cents from each one. [laughs]

MD: ...you talk about playing single kick.

Chad: For one thing, I was always a big Bonham fan, who had an amazing single kick. Also, I know that if I got a double kick, I would want to throw it in a lot because it's a new toy. I have it at home and I'm working it up, and you can use it tastefully, so maybe I'm making excuses. But it's also that on the stuff that we're doing, it's never like, "Oh gee, I wish I had a double pedal because that would be really bitchin in this part."

With the Chili Peppers, Flea plays very percussively, with a lot of slapping—not on all his stuff, but on some of it, especially the older songs—and I don't want to clutter up the bottom. I don't want to be going "diga-da diga-da diga-da" at the end of a song. That's ridiculous; it's very non-musical.

MD: You do a lot of syncopated parts with single kick. Sometimes a hard thing for drummers to get over is playing those types of things while the hi-hat is staying constant on quarter or 8th notes. Was there anything that you ever worked on as a way to free up your brain to play that stuff?

Chad: I used to practice doing triplets with straight four on the hi-hat or playing in six with my left foot and in four with my right, and then switching. These are just mental things that you have to work on to get over. I'm not totally ambidextrous, like this arm can do this while this arm does something else. Certain accents are still difficult for me. It just takes practice.

MD: Since you do a lot of quick bass drum parts, do you need to muffle your bass drum any special way to make the notes sound clear?

Chad: What I do is fold a U-Haul packing blanket once, stick it inside the drum, and put the front head on. When I tune it for live, where I also use a Remo Falam Slam impact pad, I tune the head really slack so that it's like one twist above wrinkles. If you can get used to playing with it that slack, you get a really good punch. You hear the attack really good. Sometimes the drum can sound good to you from behind the kit, but you go out front and it's not happening. So be sure it sounds good out front. That's what works for me.

MD: Anthony was saying in rehearsal that he likes the fact that you play for the song. Do you ever have to consciously make a choice as to how busy your individual parts are going to be?

Chad: Yeah, I do. Lots of times Flea and I will be jamming and coming up with parts, and we'll play off each other. In some cases, I'll simplify. Sometimes I'll just cop something in one of my limbs off of what he's doing, accenting along with him. Lots of times it'll sound too busy, so I'll have to pick out the important notes. At this point with the band, it's more about just listening to everybody. It's the whole vibe of the song and what Dave is doing, what the vocal is doing—trying to play what the song needs. I think I'm maturing a little bit more. I think I'm playing less. I'm trying to concentrate more on the groove and not about playing a fancy part so that drummers will go, "Oh, that's cool." I'm more concerned with the overall feel. Rick Rubin, who produced *Blood Sugar* and the new album, is really good at that—"That's too much, play half of that." We definitely worked on stuff more on this record than on *Blood Sugar*. We really ripped some things apart—"Okay, on the second verse you're gonna do what? Let me hear just you and Flea. Okay, now play by yourself... no, don't do that, do this...crash here...play out there...set that up, don't set that up." Rick really made a lot of good suggestions.

MD: Is it hard getting used to someone picking your stuff apart like that?

Chad: No, not if you can set your ego down a little bit. I respect him. He's real musical, real smart. He has a good concept of space. I respect his background. I don't always agree with him, and we've knocked heads a couple of times, but that's just two artists trying to see their vision through. And Flea, Dave, anyone in the band can make a suggestion. I'll always try 'em. It really helps.

MD: Getting back to the actual parts you play: We talked about the bass drum. How about the hi-hat?

Chad: I've always played the hi-hat plenty loud because I've played in so many bands where drums weren't miked, back in the backyard party days. Man, I like them loud, real sloshy. I've since curbed it a little bit. There's a certain sound to an open hat; it sounds like you're hitting.

MD: You seem to have a lot of fun playing the hi-hat; you add lots of different colors with it.

Chad: The hi-hat is amazing. There was a Gene Krupa tribute years ago. All of the drummers came out and busted their shit, man, doing all of their solos. Jo Jones came out with just a hi-hat and blew everybody away. That's the shit, man. What was it like when there was no hi-hat, when they had the low-boy? I'm a big fan of the hi-hat, more than the ride. In funk music, you can accent so well with it, with different open and closed sounds. It's definitely one of my favorite things to play. And there's nothing like tightening up on the old hi-hat in a verse to make things go "shhhhhp." It really has a lot of personality.

MD: Another thing you talked about in your video was ghost strokes.

Chad: What do you need to know? They're very spooky. Actually, they're a big part of my so-called "style," if you can say that I have one. They're really funky and they fill up stuff. You can be doing full-on doubles, which isn't really that ghosty, but there are so many different dynamic levels. When you play a straight boom-tat, 2/4 groove, it can sound kind of stiff. But if you just drop your hand in there, where you think it naturally fits in, it can make such a difference in the groove. I'll usually do it in places that have more holes between snare shots.

MD: On the other hand, rather than fill up space with ghost

notes, you sometimes seem to accentuate the space between notes by stretching the time.

Chad: On "Blood Sugar," going into the last chorus—"bam, bam, bam, blood sugar baby"— we kind of ritard that because it explodes even heavier when it comes back in. We never talk about it, but we know that we do it. It's just from playing together. There is tension and space, big time. Rick is a big fan of that too.

MD: "Mellow Ship Slinky" has that sort of thing going on.

Chad: You mean the "bomp, bomp, bomp, bomp, da dunt da dun, uh ba da dunt dunt da dah" part? I remember [former guitarist] John Frusciante was physically leaning back when we played it. I had to consciously lay back. If you lay a click track on it, it would probably drag, but the feeling of it is that it gives you that full value thing, which is cool. Then it kicks back into the swing part, "do, do, a-dack-a-do."

MD: There seems to be a jump between the last two albums, particularly in that sense; there seems to be more space on *Blood Sugar*.

Chad: For one thing we had been playing together for a couple of years by the time we recorded *Blood Sugar*. *Mother's Milk* had a good energy, but it wasn't a real relaxed energy, which I think *Blood Sugar* had. *Blood Sugar* sounds like a band playing in your living room. There are minimal overdubs. We were just trying to capture a good performance, with natural sounds. *Mother's Milk* had sampled drums, triggered shit, overdubs. *Blood Sugar* is definitely more natural, organic, which is the way we want to sound. It was a maturity in songwriting, too. There's also not the latest technology on there. It's like an old board, crappy old mic's, regular drums.

MD: What about this new record?

Chad: It's different on different songs. We were really prepared when we went in to do *Blood Sugar*. We had twenty songs together, and it was just a matter of getting good performances. This time we had about fifteen songs, but they weren't all finished. Sometimes that can be an advantage, and I think for us it was, especially with the way

Michael Bloom

Michael Bloom

Dave creates. You can use the studio as a real tool; things change when you hear them in the nakedness of a studio environment. So, it's different this time, but it's still real organic and natural-sounding.

MD: Tell us about some of the new stuff.

Chad: There's a song called "Evil," which is kind of like a ZZ-Top, boogie kind of thing. With a straight beat it would have sounded like boring rock 'n' roll. So, I do a free-jazz odyssey thing over it. It's like my interpretation of jazz on steroids. It's different, but it works. There won't be a lot of air drumming going on when we do it live. The other guys are the rhythm section and I'm sort of the lead.

I played with my hands on some songs, and we even had Stephen Perkins play with us. El Perk came down and rocked. One song, "Stretching You Out," is kind of a combo thing, where we all played together. I was playing the drums, Stephen was play≠ing all this crazy percussion stuff. "Junkie Song" was just me playing drums, Flea playing an ashtray, Dave playing the floor tom, and Stephen playing this thing called a cajon, which is like a wood box with a hole in it. Anthony sang over it, and it turned out cool. Rick loves it, he's like, "It's rad. It's the dope, it's the rope, it's the

fly." Stephen's a really good musician and a nice guy. He plays interesting stuff.

Then there's a song called "My Friends." It's kind of a Tom Petty-ish, Stan Lynch kind of feel—not really slow, but I had to play quiet and straight. The hardest thing for me is to play slow and solid with conviction. I can play hard and fast all day— no problem. But to really groove quietly and at a slow tempo...kids should put a metronome at point 2 or something and just try to make it sound really good and solid and grooving.

MD: Some drummers think in terms of 16th notes when they have to play slowly.

Chad: Steve Smith does that. I saw that in a video somewhere. Not a bad idea.

MD: Do you ever find yourself doing that?

Chad: No, I very rarely do a counting thing. Except at the Modern Drummer Festival [where Chad did several duets with percussionist Larry Fratangelo]. Larry wanted to do something in seven. I'm thinking, "All-right...this is easy, man. Think...in... seven." [laughs] But I don't really do that. I'm more listening to where other people are placing their notes than counting.

MD: Do you and Flea ever jam together as you did in your video?

Chad: Yeah, especially when Dave is late for rehearsal, like today. But coming up with parts, just me and him? Not often—it's more of a band thing. We do have two things that we recorded on the new record that just has bass and drums—a song called "The Intimidator," which didn't make it onto the album, and something temporarily called "Slow Funk." Dave didn't have a guitar part ready, and while we were in the studio we just wanted to lay it down. But usually everybody jams together.

MD: Do you get to do the sort of duets you did with Larry Fratangelo at the MD Festival very often?

Chad: That was a treat because he and I hadn't played together in a long time. We were in a band together in Detroit, where he still lives, and he was in P-Funk. We played on the Grammys together when we brought out George Clinton and the P-Funk guys. It was really fun. There were about thirty people on stage—two drummers, five bass players.... The Grammys are generally so uptight. It was nice of them to ask us to play, so we decided to pay homage to George and turn people on to some of the real funk.

MD: You've done a few sessions lately.

Chad: I wouldn't call myself a "session man." I just get lucky through friends or friends of friends. Ross Garfield, the Drum Doctor, turned me onto a John Fogerty thing. John had asked Ross for suggestions on drummers, so there's Josh Freese, myself, Nick Menza from Megadeth, Curt Bisquera, Eddie Bayers, Steve Jordan. Some of the last stuff Jeff Porcaro did is on there.

The way John works is very interesting. It was just me, him, and a bass player. We played a pretty straight-ahead rock tune like two or three times, and it sounded good. He's like, "Sounds great. Maybe just try this in the chorus," a couple other sug≠gestions. So, we went back in and did that. "Cool man, sounds great, let's break for lunch." I figure, great, we got it, now we're gonna move on to another tune, maybe a swampier CCR thing. But after lunch, it's, "Okay, we're gonna do it again." "Uh...okay." So, we did it again...and again...and again...and again—like twenty times. And I'm going, "What the hell, man?" I'm used to three or four times—if you don't get it you move on to another song.

So, we came back the next day and played it twelve more times. He was still saying, "Yeah, sounds good, man. I really like what you're doing. Let's do one more." I asked him, "Is this the way you did it back in the CCR days?" and he said, "No, we'd do it a couple of times and that was it." And I'm like, "Yeah, that seems to be the way to do it!" But he said, "Yeah, but we were a band then, and this isn't a band. If we had rehearsed for months before, then it might have been a different story."

Then I came back on the third day, and we played it five more times. I think he was finally pleased with it because we went home early. I saw the engineer a few days later and

asked him, "What did you do yesterday?" "We edited drum tracks." "Oh, cool." "Yeah, seventy edits." "Seventeen edits?" "No, seventy."

MD: How did you manage to stay fresh after all the takes you had to do?

Chad: I just had to really Zen down. I said to myself, "Okay, this is the first time I've played this." It's a long process, but he's trying to get that really special feel for the performance, and that's cool. In the end he was happy; he was a really nice guy, and I was very honored to do it. Ross told me I'm on the record, so I'm pleased.

MD: You've done other outside projects, like a Queen remix.

Chad: They wanted to put something special on the American CD release of *News Of The World*, so they had asked Rick Rubin to remix "We Will Rock You/We Are The Champions." Me and Flea just rocked out at the end of it. We put a groove to it. So that was different.

Then I did this Johnny Cash thing, which was amazing. I walk in and I'm all excited: "Hi, I'm Chad, the drummer for the Chili Peppers." "Glad to meet you. I'm Johnny Cash," he says in that voice. He was very charming, a total gentleman stud man in black. He goes, "What do you want to play?" "What do I want to play? Anything you want. I'm here for you." So, he sits down and puts on his reading glasses, goes to his folder, plays me some songs. "This is a song that Kris Kristofferson wrote for me, Chad. What do you think of this? And here's one that Dolly Parton gave me. What about this one?" So, it was pretty rad.

It was me, Flea, and Mike Campbell from Tom Petty's band. It wasn't really our thing, but it was cool. We played four or five songs—"Heart Of Gold" by Neil Young, a Leonard Cohen song, some religious songs, some train-feel Johnny Cash kind of stuff.

MD: Do you think studio work is something you would like to do down the road?

Chad: Oh God, I don't know—maybe. I like the studio. But I prefer playing music that I like and with people that I like over doing jingles and soundtracks. I don't think that's for me. The main thing about being a studio guy is probably adapting to each situation, being able to wear different hats. Like Jim Keltner—he's just such a nice, easygoing Southern gentleman, he puts everyone at ease. I'm sure that's part of why people like to work with him. He's no slouch on the drums, either. I think you have to have the personality for it and treat each situation differently.

MD: Speaking of different, you've got a new look in the photos accompanying this story. What's the deal?

Chad: I'm paying homage to the fathers of the drumset. Gene Krupa, Buddy Rich, Chick Webb, Baby Dodds, Big Sid Catlett, Ray McKinley, Jo Jones—those guys were amazing. It was such a cool time. They looked so stylish.

I think that if you're really serious about your instrument you should at least check that stuff out. Jazz swing was the rock music of the day, and those guys were like rock stars.

Gene Krupa was a teen movie idol rock star guy. He really brought the drums to the forefront. We owe him, and all those guys, a lot of nods.

MD: When did you start listening to that sort of stuff?

Chad: My dad was a little bit of a swinger. He'd break out his navy suit, "When me and your mom were kids...." [laughs] Later in high school I had a drummer friend, and we would sit and shred and listen to Santana and funk and swing stuff. The sound on some of those recordings isn't very good, but you can get the feel of what's going on. Later on, I got into it just because I wanted to know more about where the

fan. I actually went home a couple of times and played the National Anthem at the games. I met Isiah Thomas at the MTV Awards one time. He sat right in front of us. We started to talk, and he said, "Next time you come to town, do you want to play the National Anthem at one of our games?" I said, "Yeah!...but I'm a drummer," but he said, "Do whatever you want. It'll be fine."

So I got a 1960s Chicago Symphony version of the anthem—it's pretty bold, lots of horns and stuff—and I did sort of a John Bonham version, bringing it down for a section, and then rocking out at the end. They loved it. It was

Michael Bloom

instrument had come from—how the low-boy became the hi-hat, how cymbals started getting bigger. There's a cool book called *Drumming Men* [by Burt Korall] that's all about that time.

MD: Another one of your passions is sports. You mention it in your video.

Chad: I love sports, especially basketball. I think those guys are just awesome athletes. I'm a big Detroit Pistons

really exciting. I was never so nervous in my life. Usually, I've got the guys in the band running around. I went back for a playoff game and did it again.

I also like to ride my bike and go scuba diving—this is beginning to sound like *The Dating Game*. I find movies really inspiring, too. People ask me, "What do you listen to when you're in a rut?" Lots of times it's not music. I'll go to a really great movie or watch it at home—rent *Raging Bull* or a Fellini movie. Just like in music, there's balance, dark and light, dynamics, power. I get lost. I go to a basketball game, and if it wasn't for the clock, I'd be lost. That's art to me.

MD: We mentioned your book earlier. You used a drum tablature system, which is different from what most books do.

Chad: I was really pleased about that. I'm not a big technical reader guy. The drum tab is like a graph cut up into sections of quarter notes—1 e & ah 2 e & ah—and it puts a little dot in the graph right where each note falls—where the snare drum or the hi-hat or the bass drum is. So, you can just go, okay, beat number 4—that's where the snare drum is.... It makes it really simple.

MD: What sort of training did you have when you were young?

Chad: I started playing the drums when I was seven, when I was growing up in Michigan. I didn't take formal lessons, but I played in the symphonic bands, concert bands, jazz bands—any band class that would help me get an A to balance out my D in current events or biology or whatever, [laughs] I'm not an expert reader at all, but that's where I learned to read.

Later I played in bands with my brother. Since he is about two years older than me, he was a big influence on me musically because I would listen to all his records. He was into Jimi Hendrix, Led Zeppelin, Black Sabbath. Anyway, when I graduated from high school, I went right to playing in clubs. I played all kinds of stuff—rock, wedding bands, anything that I could get my hands on just to play, because I knew that's what I wanted to do.

MD: How were your parents about your career choice?

Chad: My parents were very supportive, which is great. They were a little concerned, but they were always really cool about it. I definitely have to thank them for that. If I ever got punished, I got grounded. But they would never say, "Since you sneaked out of the house and stole the car, you can't play the drums." I think that maybe I got good because I got grounded so much, [laughs] I got a lot of practice.

MD: So where did you go next?

Chad: I played in a band in '82 with Larry. He was in P-Funk right before that. He was a big help. I'd gotten to the point in my drumming where I felt that I was pretty good, but I didn't really know about dynamics and building songs. Larry was instrumental in opening my eyes and ears to that stuff.

So, we were in this band; this guy put together this supposed Detroit super group around great musicians. He owned a place called Pine Knob, which is an outdoor theater in Detroit. We rehearsed there for about a year. He didn't know anything about music, but he tried to tell us what to do and what to play. It was just a weird scene. But the good part was that I got to play every day with some really good musicians. Larry and I really hit it off, and he sort of took me under his wing. Probably my first real funk influence came from Larry. So, I matured a lot in that year.

MD: When you were playing the clubs, you must have also been learning a lot about the different aspects of playing live, like monitor mixes and sound and things like that.

Chad: It's good not to piss off the monitor guy. Sometimes at a gig you don't have time for a sound check. Lots of times I've played outdoor shows where you are winging it. But you should definitely set up your drums and get comfortable with them before they start setting up the mics so you're not moving your stuff for them. But after that, you should try to be nice so they will give you a good mix. [laughs] I just tell them I want bass guitar, kick and snare, little bit of guitar, and a little bit of vocal. Sometimes they can throw toms in. When I have my own mix I usually get the whole drumset in there—not too loud, but just so it's not like you're here and the drums are over there.

MD: What happens if you get a lousy mix?

Chad: If it's not happening, don't get pissed off and let it ruin your whole performance. I've seen guys look really upset on stage, and you're watching and wondering what's wrong with the guy. You have to bear with the situation, and hopefully after two or three songs they'll have it together. They'll usually take care of the singer first. Drummers get the shaft in that department.

In any amplified situation it's important that you hear what's going on. When I was in the band Toby Redd, I demanded a monitor. "Well, we don't have the money for it." "You want to play together? I need to hear what's going on. I have to have a monitor."

MD: What was Toby Redd about?
Chad: It was a rock band from Detroit. We put out a record on RCA, but nothing really happened. We went on a couple of tours and then we started playing the clubs again five nights a week. At this point I knew everybody in Detroit, all the bands. Eventually I thought to myself, "I don't want to be hanging around at thirty years old and still playing the bars. I'm out of here." So, it was either New York or L.A. I had

had enough of the cold weather, and my brother lived in San Francisco, so I just came out here to L.A. and went to Musicians Institute.

MD: How long were you there?

Chad: A couple of months. If I had been a kid coming out of high school, I think it would have been really good, but I was twenty-six years old. That's not to say that I was above them; there were definitely things to learn. But the semester that I went, they tried to get everybody in kind of the same place. The bummer was that it was about $4,500 to go, and after about half a semester they gave me ten percent of my money back. So on the back of *Mother's Milk* I thanked PIT for the huge refund. Now they put me in their ads— "Alumni Chad Smith of the Peppers!" But I think it's a good place—it's like a trade school. You can learn a lot.

MD: How come you decided to go there?

Chad: I just wanted to better myself. I also wanted to check out L.A. to see if this was what I wanted to do. After being there for a couple of months, I auditioned for the Chili Peppers...and now I'm rich and famous! [laughs] My mom says, "Don't you just pinch yourself every day?" But it's true, because there are guys who can do my thing no problem. I certainly paid my dues, but I'm still lucky to be able to do what I love for a living. [Chad pauses, sincerely.] Man, I am just so lucky.

Ebet Roberts

Ask a Pro
November 1995
Tuning Toms and Other Tips

I saw you at the Reading Festival in '94 with the Chili Peppers, and I immediately came to the conclusion that you are the coolest drummer I know. Here are some questions that I desperately need answered:

1. How do you tune your toms—especially on "Breaking The Girl"?
2. How do you tune your kick drum for live playing (as at Woodstock '94) versus recording (as on "Funky Monk's")?
3. During the "Give It Away" video I saw you using Zildjian cymbals, and I thought you played Sabians. What was that all about?
4. What tips can you give me for studio work?
5. What do I practice to be like you?

Max

Hey Mad Max: Today is the Ask A Pro five-questions-for-one blue-light special, so your desperation is in luck. Here goes:

For the tuning thing, it's pretty simple. The toms are tuned so that I can play the first three notes of "In the Mood" (the old swing tune, not the Rush song). My kick drum is tuned pretty much the same both live and in the studio: The batter head is just a twist up from the wrinkle stage. Add a packing blanket folded once and you're all set.

As far as the "Give It Away" video goes, you were very observant to catch a glimpse of the brand name on the cymbal. I do use Sabian cymbals, and I have for ten years. But in certain situations (like video shoots) rented gear is used—and when you're painted silver in the desert, there aren't many drum stores around.

With regard to studio work, I think you're asking the wrong guy. But I can tell you that I basically take the same approach as in a live situation: Play for the moment and give it everything you've got.

As for "being like me," I'm flattered that you like my playing, but be yourself and play what's in your heart.

Reflections
October 1997
by Robyn Flans

The unfortunate thing about having to commit a Chad Smith interview to paper is the risk of losing something in the translation. Chad's personality is animated, he's funny, and he often speaks with his tongue firmly in his cheek, so you just never know quite what he's going to say next. It's refreshing to see someone of Chad's stature within the music industry who still maintains the enthusiasm of an avid fan. Hopefully, that comes across in this interview conducted at NRG Studios in North Hollywood, California, where Chad and Chili Peppers bandmate Dave Navarro were working on their own side project.

Jack Irons
Jack played on my favorite Chili Peppers record, *Uplift Mofo Party Plan*. I really enjoyed the drumming that Dave Abbruzzese did with Pearl Jam, but I think that Jack has injected a new sort of maturity into that band, which I enjoy on their new record. Jack has always been very supportive of me with the Chili Peppers. If I ever needed to ask him how he played a certain part of a song or something, he was always cool. He's a great guy, and he has the raddest tattoos of any guy that I know. He has got some bold, bold whales on his back that are just the coolest. Jack is a very inspiring person, and a good friend.

Steve Jordan
Steve Jordan is a rock star! I really enjoy the stuff that he did with Keith Richards' band, the Ex-Pensive Winos. I saw them play and I was blown away; I thought Steve was great. I really enjoyed seeing *Hail Hail Rock And Roll*—the Chuck Berry concert movie where Chuck used Keith's band and Steve was playing. I also enjoyed watching Steve play on the David Letterman show. I thought it was really cool how he had his cymbals way up high.

That was probably not the most physically economical way to play, but it looks good.

Steve is a really solid player. He's got the old-style rock, bluesy type playing down hard, and he always has a really good popping high snare drum sound. I just think he's a wonderful musician. I don't know him personally, though.

Zigaboo Modeliste
Zig-man? Zigaboo could be one of the funkiest human beings walking the face of the earth. The playing he did with the Meters was groundbreaking. When I first joined the Chili Peppers, Anthony [Keidis, singer] gave me a Meters record and said, "Listen to this. If you can pick up anything through osmosis, this is the kind of funk we're into." That record was my first hardcore exposure to Ziggy. The feel that he has is indescribable; I don't think anyone else has it. Any musician, not just a drummer, owes it to himself to listen to the Meters and to Ziggy. He's the man!

Phil Rudd
God, Phil Rudd plays 2 and 4 like nobody else. I had the privilege to see AC/DC track their last record, because Rick Rubin produced it and we work with Rick a lot. I think Rick was somewhat instrumental in getting Phil back in the band. They had gone through some other drummers, which goes to show you how changing one person—and certainly the drummer—will change the sound of even a very simple band like AC/DC. *Powerage* is one of my favorite records; Phil's drumming goes to show that although you may be able to play a bunch of notes, what's important is being able to play 2 and 4 and make it feel like that. Phil has a definite feel in his simple way of playing. He's very inspiring to me. He and Charlie Watts, as far as playing rock 'n' roll music, are two of the guys who can play really simple with incredible taste and personality, and as solid as a rock. Phil

Tony Woolliscroft

is the man! He's the man again! He really is. He is one of the many men. [laughs]

John Bonham

That's an easy one. John Bonham is probably the greatest rock drummer who ever lived. Everybody knows it, so everyone tries to emulate his sound. But no one can do it. It's too bad that John Bonham is not alive, because I'm sure he would still be making amazing music. Bonham was very funky. A lot of people think of "the John Bonham sound" as the loud, big drum sound, so they just try to play really loud to sound like him. But John Bonham didn't just hit the drums really hard; it's how he hit them. That goes to show that how you hit the drums, and how you mike your kit, is really a big part of your sound, and he was the guy for that.

Art Blakey

He's another innovator, from the bebop era. The cool thing about Art is that he played right up until he died. But he was always staying fresh; he always wanted to know about new things. He didn't say, "Here's my jazz thing. This is what I do, and I'm stuck here." He was always growing as a musician, as all musicians should. Art Blakey and Elvin Jones are probably the two jazz guys for me. I mean Elvin was kind of the John Bonham of his time, for that kind of music.

Art Blakey was another guy whose personality came through the drums. I saw him at Catalinas two years before he died. He was so exuberant and had so much life and was so into it. He preserved and helped put out the greatest American music, which is jazz. He took it everywhere. He was also a great bandleader. A lot of people think of drummers as the guy in the back, but Art Blakey was a leader. He had a sense of humor—and that voice. He was just a character, man. I thoroughly enjoyed seeing him. Kids often listen only to what's going on today, but they should go back and listen to any records he was on. They are in for a treat if they check him out.

Tony Woolliscroft

Richie Hayward

Richie's a great guy and a great drummer. I dig his sort of unorthodox style. There is something about the way he comes up with stuff. I don't think he's a schooled guy, and you can't teach that kind of stuff anyway. I think it's the same with the drummer from Sly & the Family Stone, Greg Errico. It's not about the technical, it's the way he played and came up with

stuff that made it sound that way. I'm certainly an advocate of taking lessons and studying, but sometimes when people just play from feel and are self-taught it's very original and unique. I think that Richie is one of those guys. The way he plays sounds really original to me.

Gene Krupa

I love Gene Krupa! Drummers would simply not be where we are today if it wasn't for Gene Krupa because he brought the drums to the forefront in the '30s. Gene Krupa was kind of a teen idol, like a movie-star type guy. I mean he was handsome. A lot of his playing was overlooked because he was really into being a showman, and people focused on that. But the stuff he did with Goodman was great. He was a simple but powerful drummer. What do I like about Gene Krupa? He really had style, man. And he was another bandleader. And again, although he played until he was really old, he was really into keeping up with what was going on. He's the guy that made people pay attention to the drums.

Keith Moon

John Bonham, Mitch Mitchell, and Keith Moon were probably my three major influences when I was a kid. For Keith Moon, the drums were like a lead instrument. I had never really heard that before—certainly not in rock music. He is the guy I really think had the most personality. He was all about the show. I had never heard anyone incorporate crashes in the middle of fills. Usually, drummers crashed when they finished a fill. I thought that was really cool. Obviously, less was not more with Keith Moon, which I think was a reflection of his lifestyle as well. He was a pretty excessive guy. It's a shame that it took a toll on him.

So many drummers sound generic these days. But Keith Moon had so much personality, and you really heard it in his drumming. He had a sound and everything, but it was more the way he played and how he approached the music—not just keeping a straight little beat—that influenced me.

Stephen Perkins

Stephen Perkins definitely has his own thing, which is hard to do these days. He has a very original style. I think the drumming he did with Jane's Addiction was some of the best rock drumming in the last ten years. Obviously, since I'm playing with Dave [Navarro, former Jane's Addiction guitarist] I always get, "Well, what would Perkins do?" So, I say, "Why don't you call him and get him down here!" No, Stephen's a great guy—we're friends. He played on our last record. I love to watch him play. Again, he's a guy who's always into new stuff. He's triggering and doing crazy stuff, and he always has some crazy new setup. We're going to do something together one of these days. That could be really fun.

Matt Cameron

Matt is one of the latest and greatest. Soundgarden and the Peppers played together on Lollapalooza '92, which was a real treat. I would always get there in time for their set, because I always wanted to watch them play. Obviously Matt has a jazz background, but he still plays with conviction. He does that odd-time thing so seamlessly, which I find amazing. I would be lost. And it doesn't sound like he's playing odd time. Matt is one of the best guys going today. If I was a kid, I would listen to those Soundgarden records and play along to them because he has a really good feel.

Tony Woolliscroft

Brad Wilk

Brad Wilk from Rage Against The Machine. I think the word "Machine" is part of their band name because Brad is a machine! He hits hard. We played with them last summer at some festivals, and they played right before us. I'd go out and watch them and think, "Man, these guys are hittin'. We gotta get out there and really...," you know. It really made us want to play well, because they're a really powerful band.

I like the way that Brad plays. He plays a lot of beats with his crash. He's simple and powerful. He gets a good sound, and he's ferocious. I definitely hear John Bonham in his playing. He's fierce: When he plays, he means it, and I like that. I like to see guys with real conviction. I'm kinda from the same school, so I enjoy that.

David Garibaldi

That East Bay grease funk that he came up with really inspired me, although I got turned on to it in 1982, long after it came out. Stuff like "What Is Hip" and "Soul Vaccination" blew me away. I tried to play along with "What Is Hip," but it was like, "How is he doing that?" He took the James Brown/Clyde Stubblefield/Jabo Starks funk and did it in a whole different way. I mean people sample his stuff, and they still can't figure out how he did certain beats. I've had the pleasure of doing some clinics with him and hanging out with him, and he's a very sweet guy. I feel like such a groupie sometimes, just

picking his brain. He's always really cool.

David is definitely one of the big influences on me as far as funk drumming. He's obviously a real student of the drums, and he's another one of those guys who's always striving to be a better musician. I really admire that. When I went to make my video for DCI, they sent me some videos to study, and I thought that his were some of the best. He's really good at conveying; he's a good teacher. It's pretty funny when we do clinics, I get out there and go, "Yeah, yeah, this is what I do. I just play in this band and here it is... ba dap pssht." He's like, "Let's start on beat 4 after the "&" of 2. Okay, we're all gonna do that together now." We certainly have different styles of expressing our love for the instrument. But I suppose the balance is good.

Peter Criss

Oh man! I loved KISS when I was a kid. Not really anymore, but I liked them when I was nineteen. They were definitely influential to me, with the whole showmanship thing—the big show and the entertainment factor. I loved that. And Peter always seemed to play what was right for the song.

Their first record is the one that I like the best. "Strutter," "Cold Gin," "Fire House," all those songs. My brother used to say, "Why do you like KISS? Those guys stink. They can't play, their songs blow. You like Led Zeppelin. They're really good." I'd say, "I know, but KISS is cool, man. They breathe fire and spit blood, and they wear makeup." Besides that, Peter was the big-drumset guy. I probably liked Pearl drums because he used to play Pearl drums. So, it's actually all his fault that I'm playing Pearl.

Vinnie Colaiuta

Young Vinnie! He can do anything. And he does it with feel. He can go from the most complicated, crazy Frank Zappa stuff to groove playing with Sting. I can see why so many drummers want to emulate him, because he's so smooth and tasteful. You know, I always marvel at guys who play with such great technique, but also have really good feel. I think that he is definitely one of those guys. I would just like to rub up next to Vinnie, hopefully some of his talent would come through his pores and get onto me. Then maybe I could do some of the stuff he does, 'cause he's great.

Before we close, I'd like to add Dave Grohl. People wrote in to *Modern Drummer* saying, "Why did you put Dave Grohl in the magazine, and blah, blah, blah." Let me just say that right now, to me, Dave Grohl is the best rock drummer going. Period. ♣

Serving Up a New Red Hot Brew

The August 1999 Interview

by Robyn Flans

Happearances can be deceiving; Chad Smith is proof of that. The Red Hot Chili Peppers are known as the quintessential sex, drugs, and rock 'n' roll band. And at times, their individual profiles have fit the image. But for Smith, that image might be more fiction than fact. Don't misunderstand: Chad's definitely no choirboy. But this drummer is a fairly normal, albeit slightly eccentric, individual.

"Some people think I'm the guy hanging out of the limo with the Jack Daniels and the needle dangling out of my arm," Smith says, calmly seated in his lovely LA home. "We're definitely known for that—we've had drugs in our band and people have died. But believe it or not, I'm the normal guy in the band. Sure, we like to have fun, but there's nothing malicious intended. I've done some things in the past that might be construed by more conservative types as questionable. But you have to remember that, when people see an actor on TV who always plays the bad guy, they think he must be a jerk.

"We're entertainers putting on a show," Smith asserts. "We're serious about our music. But if we go on stage and have flames shooting out of our heads, it doesn't mean I go home at night and shoot flames out of my head while I'm drinking my Pepsi."

Smith keeps the band grounded, musically and personally. Although he enjoys his wild moments, band members know he's the one they can always count on. Chad is the foundation for the Chili Peppers' amalgamation of musical ingredients. He analogizes his role as being the force that stirs the pot, digging deep into the stew to dish up the bottom.

While he's had no real formal training to speak of, Smith's personal drumming style pays homage to such past masters as Gene Krupa and Jo Jones, mixed with a helping of rock stylists John Bonham, Keith Moon, and Mitch Mitchell. Also heavy in the Smith sauce are funkmeisters Greg Errico, Clyde Stubblefield, and Zigaboo Modeliste.

But while Chad shies away from the title of funk drummer, he gratefully accepts the appellation of "funkiest rock drummer around." Mostly he's proud that he can play the right thing for the band's varied songs, which is a challenge considering there are few boundaries to the Chili Peppers' creativity.

This barrier-breaking is obvious on the band's new release, *Californication*, which marks the return of guitarist John Frusciante. Once again, the Chili Peppers cook up a zippy gumbo varied in flavor and rich with taste. And there's Chad Smith, right in the middle, serving it up.

MD: Can you tell us about the creative process in the band and where the material comes from?

Chad: A lot of the songs come out of jams. We started writing for this album last June, in Flea's hot garage. We put our gear in there and just started playing.

MD: Does somebody say, "I have this idea, I have this riff, I have this pattern in mind"?

Chad: There isn't any one way a song comes together. Sometimes somebody will have a riff, like John will have something he was playing at home, he'll bring it in, and say, "I have this part. What do you guys think?" And other times it's just us getting together and playing off the top of our heads. Sometimes it's great and turns into a song like "I Like Dirt." Other times it sucks, and we'll just go on to something else.

MD: At what point do you abandon the process?

Chad: After about twenty minutes of playing the same groove it will probably fizzle out if it's not happening. Nobody will really say anything. If we like it, we'll say, "Let's record this," and if not we'll say, "Hey, let's work on that thing we were doing yesterday."

"Dirt" came really early on in the writing process. To me it sounded like a James Brown-ish kind of tight funk thing, and I came up with a kick/snare pattern that worked. Then we threw in some stops.

A lot of times the first thing you play, the gut feeling you go for, is the best. Yet everybody in our band makes suggestions for the other parts. You can never rule out any input because you never know what's going to metamorphose into something great. It might be, "That's cool, but why don't you try this," or "Do something on toms," or "What about some loud, ringy, washy cymbals." Everybody does make suggestions, but lots of times it will be my gut feeling of how it should sound from what those guys are playing and what will best complement the music.

MD: Did the bass or guitar dictate your idea on "Dirt"?

Chad: Probably more the bass on that song, certainly in the verses. It's not a song where I'm playing really hard. This lent itself to my being able to play something a little busier, funkier, and tighter, so I could get away with a little more snare and hi-hat things.

MD: What was the evolution of "Californication"?

Chad: "Californication" was one of the earliest things we had. We wrestled with it, even hated it, but it turned out to be one of our best things. Anthony had the words early on and we had some music to it. We struggled with the arrangement and the parts because it was kinda boring and no one was really excited about it, except Anthony. We were already into pre-production with Rick [Rubin] when John took the words home and came up with a simple guitar part for it. He brought it to the next rehearsal, and it was completely

Morrison and Wulffraat

different. He's so good at that.

When John quit the band years ago he got into drugs really bad and hit bottom, but now he's come back to the band so focused. He's been instrumental in the way this record sounds. Once he came in with a couple of new parts for "Californication" we were able to turn it into one of the best songs on the record.

MD: What about "Get On Top"?

Chad: That was another jam. I wish I could explain the creating of the parts better, but it just comes from years of listening. It's something that is so difficult to put into words. There's no preconceived idea with us. It's not, "We're going to try to write a funky song today." It's how we feel on that day. Before I came to rehearsal, I mowed the lawn, washed my car, and bought a six-pack of beer. Flea probably dropped his kid off at school, read a book, and talked on the phone. What everybody does just gets brought into the rehearsal room. It's really hard to try to explain it without sounding like an airhead—"Duh, I don't know, I just come up with it. We just jam and if it's good, we record it."

MD: Did your part for "Get On Top" come from the bass part?

Chad: No. It's so bass-heavy because there are actually two basses on it, so bass players will be pulling their hair out trying to figure out how to do that. But John had the original wah-wah rhythm guitar part and Flea and I put our parts on top of it.

MD: I suspect that when you and Flea went to add your parts, there was no conversation about it.

Chad's *Californication* Setup

Drums: Pearl Masters Custom MMX
A. 5x14 Chad Smith Signature (black nickel-plated steel) or Brady 5.5x14 jarrah snare
B. 10x12 tom
C. 14x14 floor tom
D. 16x16 floor tom
E. 16x24 bass drum

Cymbals: Sabian
1. 14" hi-hats (Flat Hats top, AA top for bottom)
2. 18.5" Chad Smith Explosion crash
3. 10" AA splash
4. 20" AA Rock ride
5. 20.5" Chad Smith Explosion crash
6. 19" China

Hardware: all Pearl, except for a DW hi-hat and bass drum pedal
Sticks: Vater Chad Funkblasters signature model

Heads: Remo Coated CS on snare with Ambassador on snare-side, clear Emperors on tops of toms with clear Ambassadors underneath, and a clear Powerstroke 3 bass drum batter

Chad: There's rarely any conversation. We've been playing together for ten years, so we just fell in. John's part is kind of busy, but very rhythmic, and I just picked out little things that Flea was playing to accent. I wanted to choose things that would propel the groove yet still leave enough space so everybody else's part could speak.

MD: Is it a conscious decision or just a natural inclination to insert your little ghost notes?

Chad: I'm a ghoster from way back.

MD: Do you remember what started that?

Chad: I'm a big John Bonham fan, and he was a ghoster. I play so many ghost notes on this record that it could conjure up spirits. You can play simply, which I try to do, and when you add ghost notes it kind of rounds out the groove a little bit, so it doesn't sound so stiff. It's not a conscious thing to put them in, it's just a personality thing. It just makes things funkier and fatter, and rounds out the groove a little more in between the backbeats.

MD: Do you actually recall when and how you incorporated that into your style?

Chad: It probably came from listening to the records that influenced me when I was young. My brother is a couple of years older and he was into Led Zeppelin, Jimi Hendrix, The Who, Black Sabbath. To me, Sabbath's drummer, Bill Ward, is like a hard-hitting jazz drummer. I saw them at the Forum, and they were awesome! But all of that must have just seeped into my subconscious. I played along with all those records.

MD: You had a kit set up in your house as a kid?

Chad: I would set up in the house, the garage, or the basement, where it was nice and loud, and I could annoy the neighbors. My mom was very supportive. She'd call to me, "I'm going shopping now. It's a good time to practice if you want." I'd bang away with the headphones on and rock out like I was playing with Zeppelin or Hendrix.

MD: You've talked about your three primary influences—John Bonham, Keith Moon, and Mitch Mitchell. Can you analyze the aspects of their playing style that have infiltrated your drumming?

Chad: I got the partying from Keith Moon. As you can see, there are ghosts. Keith Moon was the first guy I ever heard who incorporated such wild abandon. He had such personality, and it came out more in his playing than almost any other musician. No one else played like that. He was the first one I heard incorporate crashes in the middle of his fills. Live At Leeds and Quadrophenia are my favorite Who records. I don't play anything like Moon, but what really moved me was that he always sounded like he was having so much fun playing the drums.

MD: So it was his attitude that you "adopted."

Chad: Yes. It took me a while to figure out that you don't have to do little fills every four bars. When you're a young player, you want to do your Neil Peart stuff. He's famous for his solos, but what he played for the songs was the right thing. As I mature as a player—I hope—I understand more and more

that it's important to play what's right for the song rather than try to call attention to the cool little fill that I practiced at home for two weeks.

I'm not a soloist. I'm a drummer who tries to play in a way that really supports the song and the other musicians. If you don't notice me that much, but it feels good, that's the highest compliment I can get. Jeff Porcaro—and I'm not in any way putting myself in a league with him—was a master at that. He might do that one little thing at the end to take it out, but everything felt so good.

MD: You may not be out front, but the band is actually made up of four separate identities that come together to make one sound. So in a way, your individual style creates an important component to the band's sound.

Chad: We've been blessed to have great players in our band. John Frusciante sounds completely different from Dave Navarro, which changes the complexion of the band and makes the other guys play differently.

MD: So the style of each player is integral to the music that comes out, which implies that each person's individuality is noticeable.

Chad: We're each a voice in the group. I think that's what makes really great groups, because if you take one person out of the band, it just doesn't have the same magic. Led Zeppelin didn't want to play anymore after John Bonham died, and The Who was never quite the same after Keith Moon died. But I'm talking about guys who will go down in the annals of rock music as huge influences. I'm not anywhere in their league.

MD: Where does Mitch Mitchell come into your style?

Chad: I would never pretend to be a jazz player, but his playing really influenced me. Those English rock drummers of the late '60s, like Mitchell and Ginger Baker, had that Elvin Jones thing. Elvin was jazz with a little bit of rock, and those guys were rock with a little bit of jazz. Mitch Mitchell had that tight drum sound with the more jazz tuning and free-flowing, spontaneous style that lent itself to Hendrix and him playing off of each other. That really turned me on. You could hear him listening. He had huge ears.

Listening is so important because so many players are caught up in their technique—this run, or this hand/foot thing—that they forget about their ears and listening to

Morrison and Wulffraat

what's going on around them. The drummer has to hold it all together and make it feel good, so it's especially important for his ears to be big. And by the way, Mitch Mitchell was another ghost-noter. I liked his sound. It wasn't as powerful as John Bonham, but that guy could make a hell of a racket. He has a distinct personality on the drums.

There aren't a lot of drummers who have their own actual sound. Stewart Copeland does: You hear him, and you know it's him. Phil Collins has his own sound, John Bonham and Mitch Mitchell, too. These are people whose sound is an extension of their personalities.

MD: The people who don't have focused, strong personalities don't seem to have that kind of identifiable sound.

Chad: When I was in high school I loved Neil Peart. I had a chance to work with an engineer who worked on a couple of Rush records who said Peart's personality really came through the music. He's a very smart, meticulous, structured, exacting player, which is his personality.

MD: What provided the funk influence in your formative years?

Chad: I'm more of a rock player in a funk setting.

MD: You're a very funky rock player.

Chad: I'll go with that. Growing up in Michigan, probably listening to the radio and Motown, had a lot to do with it. I loved Sly & The Family Stone records with Greg Errico and Andy Newmark. Flea comes from a real funk background. He influences me, and it's a hard funk. It's not like Zig [Modeliste], it comes more from a rock base. I'm not pretending to be a funk guy who is all of a sudden going to try to play like Clyde Stubblefield.

My earlier funk experience was not just from listening. I played with former P-Funk percussionist Larry Fratangelo in a band called Pharaoh for a year. I was twenty years old when I joined the band, and Larry really helped me with the finer points of playing. He turned me onto Tower Of Power, P-Funk, and George Clinton, and really took me under his wing. That must have been where the funk seeped in.

MD: Do you recall the Chili Peppers audition, where you had to apply all that had seeped?

Chad: When I auditioned for the Chili Peppers, they were kind of a college cult band that sold a few records. I wasn't a fan of the band particularly. They were just auditioning friends of friends and I had a friend who told them, "Chad eats drums for breakfast." So when I brought my drums in to audition, Flea asked, "So, that's your breakfast?" And I'm going, "Huh?"

I set up and we started rocking. We just jammed.

Morrison and Wulffraat

I didn't know any of their songs and they didn't care. There was musical chemistry right off the bat. I was playing and yelling in the back, and afterwards Flea said, "You were the first guy who was actually leading me. Most of the other guys were waiting. You just got in there and busted out."

MD: It's that strong personality.

Chad: Love it or leave it.

MD: When you got the gig, was there anything you had to do musically to prepare for working with them?

Chad: Anthony gave me a tape of some Meters and Funkadelic and said, "This is the stuff we really like," but it wasn't like, "Play like this." It was more like, "Check this out." I was totally open to it and we definitely had musical influences in common. And I think it was more that common lust for making the best music we could possibly make. I was—and still am—pretty dedicated. This is what I wanted to do, and I was passionate about it and I think they picked up on it.

Anyway, after the audition, they left a message on my answering machine, "Okay, you can have the gig, but you have to come to rehearsal with a shaved head." I had long hair at the time. I was like, "I'm not shaving my head!" I'm much bigger than those guys and they can't hold me down. [laughs] I think that was my initiation—just to see if I'd do it.

MD: Does anybody ever have to pull you back or rein you in with the Chili Peppers?

Chad: That's more producer Rick Rubin's role. This is the third album we've worked on with him. He's softened up somewhat now, but eight years ago he was always with sunglasses and the beard and he looked like he was drinking goat's blood. He's really a big teddy bear, though, the sweetest guy—and smart and very musical.

Rick has a lot of the same influences that we do in rap and rock music, and he's our age. On *Blood Sugar* he really helped us turn our jams-meet-raps into songs. That's his greatest asset. He's not a technical guy at all: He's not an engineer-turned-producer. He just knows what he likes. We'll have ten song ideas, and we'll play them for him, and he'll give us an objective, unbiased opinion. Sometimes we butt heads, other times it might be, "I like that part, but that other part doesn't do anything for me." Sometimes we don't have lyrics and he'll say, "I like it, but I've got to hear it with the singing on it." He's really good at melding our kind of unpolished musical sections into songs and helping us get in and out of sections.

Rick has worked with great people, and because of our relationship I've been fortunate to work with people like Johnny Cash, and we got to do that LL Cool J thing ["I Make My Own Rules"] for the Howard Stern soundtrack. For us, he's become like George Martin of the Beatles—he's the fifth Chili Pepper.

MD: What would be a disagreement in the studio and how would it get resolved?

Chad: It really is a democratic situation where if somebody's playing something and one of us doesn't like it, we're very honest. We're lucky that we're not afraid to say, "I don't really like that," or "That part sucks." The worst thing, though, is to say, "I don't like it," without being able to give a reason. You always have to say why. If someone really doesn't like something, even if everyone else does, there's no reason to shove something down someone else's throat. It's never going to work anyway if somebody's not there. So we move on. We've got lots of ideas.

MD: "Parallel Universe" is a real rocker.

Chad: That's my Larry Mullen Jr. imitation. We were going to try to cut it with a click because it seemed like a song that would lend itself to using one, but it worked out without it.

MD: At the end I hear your Keith Moon influence.

Chad: It had even more on there than what's there now. That's a track where Rick Rubin said to me, "Leave that for the live version."

MD: What are you doing on "Purple Stain"?

Chad: Jamming, rocking out. The bass line just stays the same, so Flea's the drummer on it. He's holding down the bottom, so I get a chance to stretch out a little. The outro is as far as I go on this record, that's for sure. John is playing rhythm too, so I'm freed up to take the rhythm a little outside—not out out, but....

MD: You sound like you're just about to fall off a cliff, but you make it back at the very last moment.

Chad: That's a good feeling, as long as you don't take it too far over the edge, just far enough so you almost go over the cliff.

MD: What inspired your part on "Porcelain"?

Chad: The drunken kind of feeling of the tune just made me feel like we should be sitting in some dirty, stinky, dank jazz basement somewhere. It's not a jazz song—it's in three—but it's just something I thought would sound right.

MD: You used different equipment on it.

Chad: I really felt the song needed a distinctly different sound from the regular rock drumset. I used a smaller kit with a bigger bass drum, with just a few mics. We didn't use any close miking on that one.

MD: You put yourself into the dank jazz club.

Chad: Exactly. We turned off the lights and we all just vibed out. There's so much space in the song—lots of whole notes. And I've never used brushes on a Chili Peppers tune before that one, that's for sure. I'm sure no drummers will be writing in and asking about my brush technique, but it was right for the song. The cymbal was a big Sabian ride, probably 22" or 24" with rivets, and I just crashed on it. I wanted that big wash.

MD: Did you immediately gravitate toward brushes?

Chad: Yes, probably more because of the volume and also because the song sounded to me as if it should be like an old record spinning with the needle falling off.

MD: What's great is that you have the imagination to go beyond what would be considered the norm for the band.

Chad: The cool thing about our group is that there are no boundaries to what we can sound like—and there never really have been.

MD: How will your live sound and equipment differ on the upcoming tour?

Chad: I've pared down, not that I ever had a big setup. I'm

MD: What were you doing between albums?

Chad: We tried to write songs with Dave [Navarro]. We went to Hawaii like we did for *One Hot Minute* and wrote a song before Flea and Dave went on the Jane's Addiction tour, which came out pretty good. When we got back together after their tour, it wasn't a healthy environment in which to create.

MD: Don't you go crazy during the down time?

Morrison and Wulffraat

just using one rack, two floors, a couple of cymbals. That limits how crazy I can get.

MD: It can actually make you more creative.

Chad: You're right. If you don't have as many options, you have to try to do things that sound more interesting with fewer things. In this situation, I don't feel the need to have a big drumset. Most of the stuff I do is just keeping the groove—hi-hat, kick, snare—with just a couple of fills thrown in. Buddy Rich didn't have a big drumset, and he made a lot of racket. Mitch Mitchell in the early days only had a four- or five-piece, John Bonham too.

MD: Why did this record take so long?

Chad: It didn't take long once we started writing it. And then we cut the basic tracks in seven days—twenty-three tracks! Six years—and seven days! It's kooky.

Chad: Yes. The worst thing about drugs and people who do drugs is that they get consumed by them and nothing else matters. Things get done but it takes a really long time. It's so frustrating when you're around it. We recorded the basic tracks for *One Hot Minute* in '94 and Anthony didn't get around to singing on them until a year later, and that's really frustrating. I like to do stuff, but when that goes on, life is pretty much on hold.

It's very selfish of the people doing the drugs, but they don't know it at the time because they're so self-absorbed in their whole thing. It doesn't just affect the person who is doing it, it affects everybody. I used to get mad about it, but then when I really saw the disease of drug addiction and what it does to people, I just had to feel sorry for them. When you see how good things can really be and you realize you could have three albums out in that time, it's very frustrating.

I have so much invested in this band and I'm proud of it. It's part of my identity. That's not to say I couldn't do other things, but I live the Red Hot Chili Peppers. If we sucked and were playing bad music or we were just cranking it out because somebody gave us the money to make an album, that would be a different story. But I think we're a great band and I don't want to give up on it.

MD: Of the four albums you've done with the band, which are you most fond of?

Chad: My favorite Chili Peppers album is *Uplift Mofo Party Plan*, which I'm not on—Jack Irons played on that one. I think it's so great—the songs, the vibe—I enjoy listening to it over and over. Of the stuff I'm on, I like all our records.

Morrison and Wulffraat

When I first joined the group, it was a new thing, and we were recording right away. While it had a freshness and it was exciting to me, listening back to *Mother's Milk* now, well, we don't sound like a real cohesive unit. It sounds like a new thing. There's nothing that replaces the thing that happens after guys have been playing together for a long time, writing songs, hanging out, and getting to know each other, especially in a band like ours.

Blood Sugar came so easy, recording at the house, working with Rick for the first time. It sounded like a band and I think it was the first time the Red Hot Chili Peppers really captured the way we sound organically, just us playing in a room. Those songs lent themselves to being recorded that way,

and we were very prepared when we went into the studio just like we were this time.

One Hot Minute was not like that. Dave had joined and it was new again, so we were kind of feeling each other out. The record has its moments, but it's a different band. When one person is replaced, it's going to sound different. It was cool. It wasn't a bad experience, although like I said before, it was kind of frustrating that the writing took so long.

Coming together and writing *Californication* with John feels like a natural progression of where we left off with *Blood Sugar* with him, and we're lucky to be able to have the chance to do it again. There's a definite chemistry that happens with the four of us, and this record went so smoothly. When we're able to just bang the songs out and we're only concerned with trying to get good performances, it's very easy. And when it goes easy, it's fun and everybody is in a good mood.

As I mentioned, we wrote the majority of this album in Flea's garage over the summer, and in October we went into a proper rehearsal place with a PA. We spent another month writing a few more songs and working on the ones we had. Then Rick came in and we worked for another three weeks with his fine tuning, bouncing ideas, writing more stuff. Then we went into the studio at the beginning of January, and boom—seven days for the basics.

MD: Of your body of work with the Chili Peppers, can you pick a few representative tracks and give us the story behind creating them?

Chad: "Give It Away" [*Blood Sugar*] is one of those groove songs that is a good indication of who I am. It's a hard funk groove that's no-nonsense and straight-ahead. I think the drums propel the track, and it came so easy. We wrote that song so fast—it was a jam and it was done.

Another song on *Blood Sugar* I like is "Sir Psycho Sexy," which is a longer number, and it's slamming. We did a Robert Johnson cover on *Blood Sugar* ("They're Red Hot") as well, when we were recording at the house. We did it outside, up on a hill, at 2:00 in the morning with a remote truck. We put a little drumset up, it was late, and we didn't want the cops there—at least not right away—so we did a few passes at it. I ended up playing it with my hands—no sticks. It was kinda fast, and my hands were bleeding. At the very end of the song, after we stop, you can hear the cars on Laurel Canyon going by and someone yelling out their car window.

When we did "Higher Ground" for the *Mother's Milk* sessions, we had some difficulty. For some reason we weren't getting the right feel. I was doing a consistent triplet pattern on the bass drum that was crippling my calf muscle. I couldn't keep it going for the whole song, and I was pissed. The producer was coming out into the room, trying to cheerlead us to play it all the way through. Flea played naked, John played with us and then he left, and it was just me and Flea. But I couldn't get it. I finally had to leave it, but when I came back the next day we nailed it. It was the hardest track to get on that record and it turned out to be the most popular, so you never know. Some of the drums are triggered, which works okay for that track, but it loses the dynamics of my playing.

MD: Speaking of dynamics, what did you do to develop that aspect of your playing?

Chad: Larry Fratangelo helped me with that. I think before then I would just concentrate on keeping good time and power my way through a song. We were in an eight-piece band and rehearsing, and sometimes it would just get out of control because there were no dynamics. Larry said, "Chad, you have to get the band's attention. They have to be listening to you, so after the solo, we're going to bring it down and that first beat needs to be really soft, so they have to listen."

MD: So it's not necessarily the loudest guy who gets heard.

Chad: Exactly. Larry said, "You've got to reel them in." Up until then I had just played the songs, and it was the louder the better. But when we added more pieces to the puzzle and everybody wanted to be heard, the next thing we knew it was just a wash of sound with no dynamics. He definitely helped me with that concept, and that's just about being a good musician and a good listener.

The drums are a big dictator of dynamics. The easiest thing for me to do is to play hard and fast. The hardest thing is to play slow and quiet. To be solid, consistent, and quiet takes great control. Larry's suggesting that in that band situation made all the difference. I still remember we were playing Tower Of Power's "What Is Hip?" and after the solo everyone went to wail. Larry said, "Listen to how Garibaldi doesn't come in right away with the snare on the 2. He waits 'til the next bar."

MD: What would you say are your strengths and weaknesses?

Chad: I think I have good ears—I'm a good listener, which is so important. On a more personal level, I think one of the strengths I bring to the group is a certain balance. If too many guys are way over the edge, too nutty, or too eccentric, it makes for an impossible situation. I think I bring a kind of grounding to the group. They know I'm always going to show up, I'm always going to perform to the best of my ability, and when they look back there, I'll be banging away, and everything will be okay. Uncle Chad is there, and they

can count on me.

As for weaknesses, I think I'm pretty lazy. I could definitely work way harder at being a technically better drummer. I have a big house and I don't have a drumkit set up—it's ridiculous. This is a lame excuse, but I just enjoy playing with people so much more than playing by myself or practicing. It's definitely a lame excuse.

MD: Any musical regrets?

Chad: I've been fortunate because I've known what I've wanted to do since I was a little kid. Right out of high school I knew I didn't want to go to college, I wanted to play music. So I went right into playing in clubs and bars. At the time I may not have been happy when I was banging it out in those Detroit clubs doing three sets a night, six nights a week, making no money, and wishing I could be in a big rock band. But I'm so happy now that I did that at the time because it

really honed my playing. I wouldn't trade those experiences for anything. When the opportunity came to be with the Chili Peppers, I was ready.

I've been in the band for ten years, and I feel so fortunate. For one thing, most bands don't last ten years. I'm in a band that I enjoy playing in and one where I'm a part of the creative process. I'm so fortunate to be able to do what I love to do, to make a living at it, and to be in a group that I think makes great music. I can't have too many regrets on the musical side of things.

I can't think of another living band I'd rather be in. Sure, I'd like to play in Led Zeppelin or with Jimi Hendrix. But from a musical standpoint, this isn't a bad gig.

Ask a Pro
April 2005
Organic Time

A our timing on the Chili Peppers' *Blood Sugar Sex Magik* is flawless. Did you use a click track while recording that album?
Nal

Thanks for the compliment on my time. We didn't use a click track on that record or on any of our records. We like the songs to groove organically, and we want them to feel as good as possible. We all play at the same time in the same room, looking at and locking in with each other. I've found that that's the best way to capture the magic on tape. Of course, it also helps if the other players have good time as well. It's everyone's job to give the song a great feel.

Ask a Pro
July 2010
Blood Sugar Snare Tone

I love the popping snare tone you get on Chili Peppers records and on Glenn Hughes's *Music for the Divine*. Can you tell me the drum, heads, and tuning you used to get the snare sound on *Blood Sugar Sex Magik*? Did you use the same choices on later Chili Peppers records and with Glenn Hughes?
Brian

The snare drum is a very important voice in your drumkit. I hadn't really found my voice until *Blood Sugar*. The drum I used on that record was a '70s-era 5x14 Ludwig Black Beauty with a Remo coated Ambassador head. The tuning was very tight, hence the high "pop" you referred to. I like that sound, as it cuts through well and adds an exciting personality to the songs. On more recent records, I've been using a variety of deeper brass snares, but I still crank them up pretty tight. With the extra depth, I can get good tone and body along with the pop.

That said, it all depends on the music you're playing, the room you're recording in, and who's twirling the knobs behind the desk. All of that will be part of the end result. Oh, I almost forgot...and you! You're the most important thing. So always be yourself. That sounds the best.

Past Wisdom/ Future Magik

The June 2006 Interview

by Adam Budofsky

Most bands who tough it out for twenty years in the modern music industry would be happy getting the occasional video on MTV2 and playing mid-size summer tours. Being able to demand top-notch support from their label, automatic interest from the press, and rabid fandom from the public…well, that's a rarefied position indeed.

Not only do the Red Hot Chili Peppers fall squarely in that second group, they've retained their artistic integrity and sheer creative edge along the way. This was made abundantly clear to *Modern Drummer* this past January, when Chili Peppers drummer Chad Smith invited us into his home to listen to a batch of songs from their upcoming album, *Stadium Arcadium*. If the tracks we heard were any indication—and there's no reason to believe they're not—this album is going to be a monster.

Spread across two discs and twenty-eight songs, the Chili Peppers' new opus shows a band maturing in all the right ways—and retaining enough youthful energy to give a band two decades their junior a good fright. As Chad points out, this is largely guitarist John Frusciante's statement. With startlingly unique six-string solos on almost every track, played through a kaleidoscope of tones and timbres, *Stadium Arcadium* is an absolute milestone for the band, a masterly web of cool ideas, slamming beats, and intense lyrical concerns. It's also a very live-sounding collection, the result of the band attempting to record basic tracks all at once, in the same room. Eventually Frusciante moved his amp into an adjacent room, but he, Chad, and bassist Flea continued ripping it up just a few feet from each other, proving that the wisdom of the past can still inspire the magic of the future.

As for the drumming, well, fans of Smith's way around a ghost note and old-school rock thunder won't be disappointed— but they might be surprised. Our ears perked up right from the get-go, as Chad's upside-down beat on "Readymade" added a whole other vibe to the cut—and still

made musical sense. And by the way, he played the *crap* out of that Bonham/James Brown concoction. Elsewhere, skewed disco beats (no kidding) and Chad's usual flair for mid-tempo, digging-in-the-dirt snare/kick/hat explosions bring back the old heat. At one point we turned to see Chad, sitting on his family-room rug, eyes closed, head-rocking along to the music like a kid deep in sleep, dreaming of being on stage with Led Zeppelin in Madison Square Garden. Two seconds later, we noticed we were head-rocking too and didn't even realize it. That's what music is supposed to do.

The secret to the Chili Peppers' success is really no mystery at all. When real artists get together to make noise in the spirit of brotherhood, communication, and truth-seeking, amazing things can happen. The individuals in this band have certainly gone through some heavy stuff, and they are definitely not the people they once were. But they've retained their respect for each other and haven't let stardom deplete their well of real old-fashioned inspiration.

Chad has added to his own suitcase of musical ideas by continuing his interest in playing on projects outside of the Chili Peppers. Notably, he's been acting as home-studio owner/drummer/producer on ex-Deep Purple singer Glenn Hughes' new album. In fact, we can hear Glenn in the next room doing vocal overdubs as we conduct the interview. Perhaps even more telling, Chad also recently finished recording the new Dixie Chicks disc. Smith might have been called in to "just be himself" on the neo-country superstars' latest offering, as producer Rick Rubin assured him, but you know he left that whole situation with some interesting new experiences and skills.

We begin our interview wondering if Chad is aware of his particular strengths as a drummer, and what he feels he brings to new musical situations.

Chad: Well, I wouldn't say I'm really good at anything. [laughs] I do feel that I have my thing I do, my own style I guess you could say. Before, I would try to change my style depending on who I was playing with. I still do that a little, like with Glenn Hughes: "I can get some of my Keith Moon in there!" When I do that I feel like I'm overplaying, but he's like, "No, I love it," so I must be making him happy. And those are my roots.

But I found it interesting going from the Chili Peppers record to the Dixie Chicks record, which I did right after. it's completely different music, but that's when I noticed that I kind of have this thing I do. it's clean—not clinically precise, but I try to hit hard, play with dynamics, and play to the song—though that's probably just from years of playing and trying to be a good musician.

The other thing is recording. I used to listen back to takes and one would be good and the other three would be all over the place, whether it's the time, or playing the wrong thing, or getting red light fever—playing nothing like you play, or not being in the moment. I don't feel nervous anymore. I'm no Jim Keltner—not every take sounds like a record—but I do think I'm getting better. I used to cringe years ago. There's some stuff on *Mother's Milk*…I loudly strike up a conversation with somebody when that thing comes on. [laughs] "So! Did you see that game?!" But I'm getting more consistent in that way.

MD: Is it also about understanding what you want to get across on a song, rather than simply, "I'm in a rock band, so I need to rock"?

Chad: Absolutely. It could be about changing the sound. Like this song we were doing yesterday: Hearing the song before I played anything on it, it sounded like a Beatle-y, Ringo-ish thing. I'm not going to sound like Ringo—nobody does— but I might put more dampening on the drums, or change to a bigger snare drum, because I felt that the song would benefit from that sound. And it kind of makes you play differently when you change things. Part of this is about engineering, but some of it comes from you.

So that's a big part of it now: being sensitive to what you think, and to the artist as well. The drums are such an important part of the song. You have to play with confidence. You have to own the drums, man. Because if you're unsure about things, the mic will pick that up. If you make a mistake, make it big! If you're a bear, be a grizzly on that mistake. If I mess up, I do it twice. Now it's a part. [laughs] And sometimes you make a mistake and you're like, I didn't mean to play over the bar, but it sounds really good.

MD: Lately you've made it a point to showcase some of the players you were inspired by growing up, such as the studio-legends feature you spearheaded in this month's issue, as well as the clinics you've been doing with Deep Purple drummer Ian Paice.

Chad: Growing up, I would never in a million years think I'd be making records with Glenn Hughes or doing drumming events with people like Bad Company's Simon Kirke and Ian Paice, and having them say, "I really like the way you play." That's amazing to me. The cool thing is the young people who enjoy what I do and come out to see me might not normally be exposed to players like them. I think it's important that they learn the lineage. I wouldn't be doing what I'm doing if it wasn't for this guy or that guy, and there's millions of them that I'd be able to say that about. And from a purely selfish standpoint, it's an excuse to hang out with my heroes and ask them what it was like being on the Starship jet or whatever, or to hang out with Jim Keltner and just soak it up. I love that stuff.

MD: What do drummers most often get wrong when they're trying to rock, or be funky?

Alex Solca

Chad: You can't really *try* to be anything. You have to do what the music calls for, but first and foremost you have to be yourself. You have guys like Stewart Copeland or Phil Collins, and you know when you hear them that it's them. Even if they play different kinds of songs, or with different people, their personalities still come through. That's the pinnacle. The individuality of any instrument is what makes people latch onto a song and what makes them like it—or dislike it. At least you're getting a reaction. There's nothing worse than, "It's okay." I don't want to be "okay." If you believe in it, people pick up on that. I think our band has a sound; we make a statement.

People tend to focus on the heavy metal guys with the fast double bass chops, but there's great guys in every genre of music. Some people are like, "Oh, I don't like country music." Well, go listen to Hank Williams or George Jones or Merle Haggard. That drumming is authentic and soulful and moves

people and makes those songs great. Those blues guys, like Buddy Guy—Hendrix wanted to be those guys. It all comes from somewhere.

I'm not saying there's not new guys doing it, but I try to go back to Chuck Berry and early guys like that. I can't play like a really good country player. But I can incorporate what their thing is, how they're approaching the music and the feeling. It's really about copping the feeling. It's like when I was younger, I'd listen to Led Zeppelin and Van Halen records, and I'd play along, and it was like I was trying to be that guy. I can't be that guy, but I want to try to get into that vibe of what he was doing.

MD: What's the easiest way to make a musical companion feel comfortable?

Chad: With the Dixie Chicks we had like eight people tracking at once. Luckily it was all talented people, like Mike Campbell from Tom Petty's band. But I was coming in cold.

In situations like that, you go with your gut feeling almost all the time. This was straight-ahead pocket. Every song has its right tempo, especially to sing to. If the singer has to rush or drag, you're screwed. So I always make sure that when we're cutting something, Anthony sings to it.

Besides that, make a good vibe, make sure everybody's happy to be there, and talk. It's very social. You want everyone to be comfortable, because if they're comfortable, they're going to play relaxed. You can't come in like, "Hey, I'm the man!" You just have to serve the song and do what they want you to do.

I didn't play anything that I didn't think was right, but because they wrote the songs, they had a vision, and I had to respect that. In our band, we write everything together, and I know where it came from—though I'm always willing to try anything. You can't get your hairs up if somebody wants to change something. You won't know unless you try it. It might be the stupidest suggestion. You know, "Do something on the toms." I'm a drummer guy, so I go right to the hi-hat. You have to be open. Rick Rubin's really big about that: "It might suck, but just try it for me, I just want to hear it." And you never know what kind of doors that opens creatively. Don't be stuck on this really cool part you came up with at home and really want to fit in somewhere. You have to be open.

MD: Did you find yourself playing different kinds of grooves with The Dixie Chicks? They're not ultra-traditional.

Chad: No, they're not, and on this record it kind of sounds southern California, Sheryl Crow-ish. But I did some waltzes! I didn't say it, but I was thinking, I don't do foxtrots. [laughs] The last time I did that was seventh grade dance class. But they're cool songs…there was this Irish-sounding thing too. But I surprised myself a little. And it's great having new

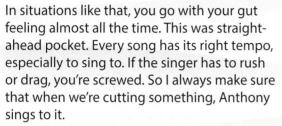

"You have to play with confidence. If you're unsure about things, the mic' will pick that up. You have to *own* the drums, man."

Alex Solca

challenges. Going in, I was a little nervous. Not that I thought I wouldn't be able to do it, but it's just like going to a new school; everybody wants to fit in. But Rick was like, "They want to rock up a little bit. You'd be good, come on down." So when I was preparing to bring my drums down there, I was like, "What should I bring?" And Rick was like, "Just be you, I want you to sound like you." Which was really cool, a nice compliment actually.

MD: Did you study up on their records?

Chad: I probably heard one or two of their songs, but I didn't go back and research them. You have to bring your own thing to the table. If they wanted it to be like those older records, they would have gotten the old guy. Unless that guy's dead [laughs] and you're replacing him specifically to sound like him. But that would be like me wearing a suit or something. I don't wear suits. It won't sound right, so get the guy with the suit.

MD: Let's take the different elements of the drumkit and talk about any obstacles you've had to get past in your development as a drummer. Let's start with the hi-hats.

Chad: For me, the kick, snare, and hi-hat are the holy trinity of the drumkit. With rock and funk, the hi-hat is the thing that the most notes are played on, and it's the lead timekeeper on the kit. Plus, there's so much personality you can get out of it, not only the dynamics, but the rhythms that you play, and what you can do with your foot—closed, not closed, in between. It has so many possibilities.

I was a real rock player growing up, a real basher, so my hi-hats used to be really big and open and sloshy all the time. In 1982 I played in a group in Detroit called Pharaoh that had some the best players in the area. I was twenty years old and I knew the leader's son from high school, so I got picked for the band. The other guys were like, "This guy's a hack, man," these very accomplished North Texas State guys. But the percussionist was Larry Fratangello from P-Funk, and Larry kind of took me under his wing. He was like, "Here's some Tower of Power records, learn how to play this."

Larry and I would ride together to rehearsal every day, and we'd listen to all this great music in the car. He turned me on to a lot of funk stuff, and he explained the way that those guys would play the hi-hat—the dynamics, when to open it up right before you go to the chorus, and barks and accents you can do with it. Before, I was banging away on it like it was just another cymbal. He also taught me when to do a fill, when not to, how to use toms in my beats, how to think of the kit as one big instrument, keeping time, listening—just musical stuff. I think I was a drummer up until then, and then I became a musician. He's a first-call percussionist in Detroit now and teaches a lot.

MD: The snare drum.

Chad: The snare drum is the most recognizable voice in the drumset. Like, if it's Stewart Copeland, you'd know it from the snare sound. I used to really analyze snare sounds. I'd go back and listen to those drummers and those records that I love from the early '70s, like Ian Paice, and they had that kind of tight, more jazzy tuning. Bonham's snare drum was tight, although it was a big drum. And I like that. But I couldn't get that sound because I just didn't know how to do it, and I had these bigger drums.

I think once I got into the metal drums and the brass drums and the smaller sizes, I found my sound. When we did *Blood Sugar Sex Magik* I used mainly this 5" Black Beauty. When you find a drum that sounds really good, it makes you play better. The snare is the drum you're playing all the time. That's the backbeat, that's what people are dancing to, and that's what the band hears. It's what pushes the track.

When I got in the Chili Peppers, we were doing a lot of fast, funky stuff, like James Brown on speed. And in order to really cut through, and because of the way I played with ghost notes, I used a Pearl free-floating piccolo drum, which wasn't bad. Really cutting. But there wasn't a lot of body to it, so I settled on a 5" drum, and that seems to be versatile enough. I like just a little higher pitch, and the smaller drums give you that. So that's kind of where I'm at right now. On the Glen record, which is more rock, I ended up using a bigger drum, a 6". I used that on the Dixie Chicks album too.

MD: With ghost notes, do you find that it's best if you're not thinking too much about them?

Chad: Yes. I hardly think about it at all. It's just really an extension of how I play a groove. Unless I'm really trying to articulate those notes, then I would think about it. But in general, just playing a straight 2 and 4 groove, I don't think about what my left hand is doing in between. I don't know if it's a good thing or a bad thing, it's just being natural. I just like the way that sounds. Sometimes Rick will say, "What's all that? You've got to cut that stuff out." I understand what he means, because sometimes it can be too much. It all has to be in the context of the music.

MD: Something I've been thinking of lately in my own playing is finding certain fills that I might just retain for a particular song. Because my tendency is not to plan things, which I'm trying to change a little. So now maybe I'll do a variation on one basic fill, rather than just splattering different ones all over the place. Do you think about that?

Chad: At first I'm just thinking about coming up with a part that will complement the other instruments or the vocals, not so much the variations. Then, going to the second chorus doesn't necessarily mean you have to play more, but rather give the impression that it's a bigger deal this time, maybe leading into the solo. You want to let people know, Here comes the solo! That's exciting. It's about building the song and trying to keep it interesting for the listener. Something new happens, and hopefully you can do it without being distracting. That's the only issue: You don't want to step on anybody.

I'm not a Neil Peart all-thought-out kind of guy. I'm more like you, I just kind of go for it and see what happens. When you're recording, you can go back and listen to it, and you might think, "Hmmm, maybe I should do less" or "maybe I should do more" or "maybe I can serve the same purpose

with just one snare shot," and leave some space. And that tension makes it exciting. Just from being in the studio and having experience with that, I think I've become pretty good at that.

Sometimes it's about playing as musically as you can, but then at other times it's about just rocking out and the raw excitement of playing something that's kind of off the wall. That can be really cool too, because you get, "Wow, that dude's really

Alex Solca

going for it." I like that too. I like people who take chances.

MD: What about tempos? At this stage, are they still an issue?

Chad: I'm the one that makes sure the tempos are right. I've got this little Tama metronome thing. That way the guys are confident that the tempo's right. You can end a lot of arguments with that. And then they feel confident when they're playing it, even if they're thinking, "This feels slow tonight," which sometimes happens when you play live every night. Maybe I laid around all day in the hotel: "Oh, this is too fast." No, this is where it is.

MD: I had a strange experience with tempos recently at a gig. I thought there were a couple songs that I started off too slow. So after the show I was going to apologize to the guitar player, but before I could he was like, "It was a really good show tonight. The tempos seemed really on." And I'm thinking, "Okay, I'm not going to say what I was going to say."

Chad: You never know, man. It is a weird physical phenomenon. When you play every night on tour, and you're like eight months in and you keep playing the same songs, they can really get a little out of whack. Taping is great, if you can stand to listen to it and take the time to go through the tapes. The songs that I don't start, if Flea or John are a little off, I can look at them and kind of give them the old, This is where it's at. I try not to make it too obvious, but it's all part of playing live, which is great. Otherwise, you have to play with a click. Screw that.

MD: Another thing I struggle with is "jumping on the train," you know, when the drums come in after the song starts, and doing it without affecting the tempo, especially with slower songs.

Chad: Yeah, absolutely. It's harder to play slower tempos in general, just to make them feel confident and solid. Anybody can play fast. You can get away with it. The more space, the harder it is.

MD: You don't always want to have a hi-hat thing going in those situations, so I try to keep some part of my body

Michael Muller

moving in time.

Chad: I think your body should be moving all the time. It teaches your limbs to talk to each other, and to do the same thing in certain grooves. I do the same thing when I'm getting ready to count something off. I'm not stiff. I get everything moving. I think it's just like revving your engine. You don't want to stop cold and then step on the gas. So, yeah, I would move something— your head, your neck. You

Chad's *Stadium Arcadium* Kit

Drums: Pearl Reference series
A. 5x14 20-ply maple/birch snare
B. 10x12 6-ply maple tom
C. 14x14 6-ply maple/mahogany floor tom
D. 16x16 6-ply maple/mahogany floor tom
E. 18x24 8-ply maple/mahogany bass drum

Cymbals: Sabian
1. 14" AAX X-Celerator hi-hats
2. 18.5" Signature Explosion crash
3. 21" AA Rock ride
4. 20" AA Rock crash
5. 19" AA China

Sticks: Vater FunkBlasters

Heads: Remo clear Emperors on tops of toms, Ambassadors on bottoms, CS Coated Black Dot on top of the snare

don't have to look like you're air drumming back there, just get into the feel.

MD: Can you recall any difficult musical lesson you had to learn on a gig?

Chad: I did a session with Fishbone, and it was with Billy Bass, who was the bass player for P-Funk for a long time. So it was three bass players: Flea, Billy Bass, and Norwood. And it was me, a percussionist, three guitar players, a keyboard player, horns…there were like ten people. This was at a studio in Venice. I was in this upstairs loft space where the drums were, which was kind of odd. Everybody was on the floor and I was upstairs looking down on them. There was no ending to one particular song, it was just like a fade-out. So I'm playing and everyone's rocking, and we get to the end of the song, so I stop playing. Billy Bass looks up and goes, "What are you doing?! Don't you ever stop until I stop!" And I was like, "Oh, shit!" I was really chastised, in front of all these people. He really let me have it. I was embarrassed. Flea is looking at me like, "Man…look at Billy Bass, don't screw around." And believe me, the next track we did, there was a twenty-minute ending, my friend. The tape ran out. [laughs]

MD: You mentioned in the liner notes of *Greatest Hits And Videos* that the band would hopefully be remembered for more than just "the socks." Ideally, what would you like to be remembered for?

Chad: That we played music that was from our hearts, and that we were honest and passionate and that we are music lovers…. And that we persevered and stayed together twenty-plus years. That's a long time for a band to do what they do and still be relevant. We're very fortunate.

I'm With You
The October 2011 Interview

story by Adam Budofsky

Nearly thirty years after embarking on his life's journey as a professional drummer, the bombastic one is at the top of his game, getting busy with the Chili Peppers, Chickenfoot, Kid Rock, and his beloved Meatbats.

When you do the math, it's almost shocking to realize that Chad Smith's searing live performances and deceivingly nuanced recordings with the Red Hot Chili Peppers have been influencing drummers for an entire generation. "Chad spawned a whole breed of "deliberate' drumming," is how Michael Miley of supreme soul-rock band Rival Sons puts it. "Drumming with intent, as if your life depends on it. He's embedded his feel in all of our minds."

Equally remarkable is the scope of Smith's influence. "One of my favorite grooves of all time is from the song 'Blood Sugar Sex Magik,' says future-groove monster Mark Guiliana, a favorite among jazz heavyweights. "It's simple and supportive yet very recognizable. I think this groove epitomizes Chad's playing—confident and creative, with a great feel that always serves the music. But I think Chad's most profound influence on the drum community is simply that he has made people want to play the drums. That was certainly the case for me. He was one of the first guys I saw play and thought, *I want to do THAT*. Chad was my first drum hero, and every time I've seen him play, I've been reminded why I started playing drums in the first place."

While his punch-in-the-gut grooves might still be the first thing people think of when his name is mentioned, at least two other equally important aspects of Smith's playing have emerged of late: his ace studio-cat qualifications, and, on the other side of the spectrum, his bona fide shredding abilities. Smith's intelligent approach to songcraft has always been evident on Chili Peppers productions, perhaps most clearly on the band's kaleidoscopic new album, *I'm With You*. But the drummer's appearance on recent recordings by the Dixie Chicks, Brandi Carlile, and Kid Rock prove that Smith can listen and support on the level of rock and pop's great session players, in the mold of his heroes Hal Blaine and Earl Palmer. For the most part leaving the slinky syncopations on thes helf, in these more conventional environments Chad provides a foundation that's solid and familiar but never cold or predictable.

Meanwhile, a pair of albums each by former Deep Purple singer/bassist Glenn Hughes, hard-rock supergroup Chickenfoot (featuring guitar god Joe Satriani and Van Halen exes Sammy Hagar and Michael Anthony), and instrumental jazz-rock quartet the Bombastic Meatbats have given Smith a chance to "appropriately overplay" in ways that would be unimaginable and, frankly, *not* appropriate on a Chili Peppers record.

"Here's the thing about Chad," says Foo Fighters drummer Taylor Hawkins. "What he plays in the studio—what you hear on record—is always pure and pristine, delivered by a serious marksman. It's when he's unleashed live, in front of an audience, that the beast takes over. He's a serious and fearless player who goes for anything. Reckless abandon takes on a whole new meaning when Chad sits down at the drums."

Yet despite the profound control he displays on sophisticated pop records, and as much as the music on recent Rock-with-a-capital-R releases allows Smith to get in touch with his inner teenager—the kid who spent countless hours playing along with Black Sabbath, KISS, and Bad Company records—the Chili Peppers are still where his heart, soul, and creative drive reside.

Ash Newell

The last time *MD* spoke with Smith, it was at his L.A. home, where he had us over to hear tracks from the as-yet-unreleased Chili Peppers album *Stadium Arcadium*. The occasion now is the release of *I'm With You*.

The album's songs, which feature the band's new full-time guitarist, Josh Klinghoffer, along with founding members Flea (bass) and Anthony Kiedis (vocals), are practically bursting with influences previously unheard on the group's records. This is bold new Chili Peppers music—adventurous, intense, immaculately crafted, and ingeniously pieced together. Across the board, Chad Smith is giving his all—and once again he comes out the other side a better drummer.

MD: When did you start working on the new music, and where did some of these new influences come from?

Chad: We started in October of 2009 and wrote songs for almost a year. There was a break when Flea went on tour with Thom Yorke and when Flea and Josh went to Lagos, Nigeria, with Damon Albarn from Blur. They went for a week and played with the local musicians. I think it was a really good bonding experience for them, and they came back with some ideas that turned into songs.

MD: "Ethiopia" is in seven.

Chad: Yeah, though the chorus is in four. It's not like we're all of a sudden playing African music, but it is different for us. I wanted to make it feel…you know how an odd-time Soundgarden song doesn't sound too proggy? Joshua Redman played sax on the outro too.

MD: With every new album of yours, the textures become more interesting.

Chad: We try. You gotta keep changing; can't keep on making the same record over and over. It's still the same guys—well, mostly. But it's got to be real, it's got to be honest.

MD: How were the drums miked for this album?

Chad: [Engineer] Greg Fidelman had thirty-two mics on the drumset—room mics, two sets of overheads, close mics, mics that are like four feet away from the kit…. You're only really listening to about eight mics at a time, but it's covered sonically. Rick Rubin likes the sound to be real preset—very little room. That's always a fight, but you have to trust people, and we have the best guys.

They'll be like, "As soon as we turn up the overheads a little bit, it gets harsh and washy." You think, *It's easy—just turn up the volume and it'll be good*. But it's not that simple. For each song,

in little ways, there has to be an adjustment because of the way the drums fit into the rest of the track. When there's a lot going on, you have to tighten up the drums, so they poke through. The tape doesn't lie.

Ash Newell

MD: Does gear choice come into play here?

Chad: Yes. Lots of times with the Chili Peppers, we had three different snares with different tonal colors, and I'd pick what I thought would work the best for a particular track: This song is faster, or it's got a quicker delay, so I'll use the higher-pitched snare. Or this one is slower, so I'll use a bigger, meatier one. But then we'll listen back and decide another snare might fit in the track better. That happened with the Kid Rock album. My snare drum is usually a higher, crackier sound. The first day we were playing, the track was sounding good, but Bob [Kid Rock] comes in and says, "Hmm, the snare is too high. I donít really like that sound."

So they had this other drum—big, deep, wood, tuned way down, tape all over it, like that '70s *duh* sound. So, we put that up: "Yeah, that's the sound!" And it made sense. Bob's going for that Southern rock, Bob Seger thing. But it was so weird to be playing that soup bowl, where I'm used to that *bing* sound and ghost notes. You just have to adapt to it.

MD: Do you have a basic way that you dampen the drums?

Chad: There are so many variables, but in general I use very little tape, and it's usually on the floor toms, which tend to ring more, and sometimes not in a good way. Sometimes it can be good, but other times you can't tell where the drums are in the mix—it muddies it up. One time when we were recording the new Chili Peppers album, I was saying, "I want it to sound like *Blood Sugar Sex Magik*." Whenever that record comes on, I'm like, "The drums, I love it!" But there's nothing else on that track but bass, vocals, and guitar. Sonically there was room for that drum sound; the territory wasn't taken up.

For this record I was like, "I want the drums to sound more like that—when it's appropriate." It's funny, because Rick loves Led Zeppelin and John Bonham. No one can get that sound now,

Ash Newell

and it wouldn't sound right with our music anyway, but something kind of in between this [taps on the table] and *ba-boom!* would be cool. And Josh, being a drummer, he'd say to Greg or to Rick, "You were there when we were recording it. You see what Chad is doing to the drums, how he's playing. The guy's six-three and he's beating the shit out of the drums. It should sound like that, not *dit…dat*." And I'm like, "Yeah, what he said! The new guy, yeah—I like this kid!" [laughs]

But there is something to that. We're a rock band, and we're trying to replicate what it sounds like when we're playing together. When we're mixing, they're probably like, "Okay, here comes Chad with his thing…." I should probably wear a T-shirt that says, "Sounds great, drums can be louder, more room sound." [laughs] But drummers shouldn't be afraid to make their voices heard. Just because you're not the songwriter or producer or engineer, at the end of the day, nobody knows what went into the record. All they hear is the end result. It's not "Rick Rubin and the Chili Peppers." It's not "Greg Fidelman featuring the Chili Peppers." It's the Red Hot Chili Peppers. So whatever people are going to hear, they're going to think that's what we wanted it to sound like.

It's your responsibility. It's not about being a prima donna or being difficult—it's your right and responsibility. You're never going to be completely happy, but it's up to you to make it the best you can.

MD: Though this is Josh's first album with the group, he's toured with you before. Will you be bringing in another musician on the next tour to sort of take his old role?

Chad: We might bring a utility guy. There's a Brazilian percussionist in New York named Mauro Refosco, who tracked about half of the new songs with us. He played with Flea in Thom Yorke's band Atoms for Peace. One of the things he has is this tree of high-pitched Brazilian drums, four on each side. He made the thing himself, and it's got levers connected to these kind of like plastic Blastick things. It's the coolest sound. Tracking with him was fun, so he might be playing with us live.

MD: You're playing some fresh-sounding things on *I'm With You*—Badfinger-ish piano ballads, Pink Floyd–like spacey sections, a soca-type groove. One constant is your hi-hat foot, which almost seems to have a mind of its own. How conscious are you of your hi-hat foot while you're playing?

Chad: I don't really think about it. My left foot is always moving around. Of course, sometimes I'm consciously keeping it closed or opening it at certain times, but when I'm just playing, it moves a lot. It sounds human.

MD: Listening to the new tracks, it's obvious that a lot of thought went into the arrangements. You all seem to get progressively better at identifying what's unique about each song and highlighting those aspects.

Chad: Well, hopefully it's about growing and improving. There was a point where the Chili Peppers were kind of a good groove and a rap, and hopefully it went somewhere. *Mother's Milk* and *Blood Sugar* were twenty years ago. Not that we don't want to do certain things like we used to, but we want to do other things as well. We try to get enough things in there without alienating the listener. It's gotta have a good melody and all the other things that make a good song. But we want to make it interesting for the listener and put things in there that you'll pick up on.

A lot of it is Arrangement 101 stuff. Something is introduced in the second verse, like a shaker or a background vocal, to keep the listener engaged and make things more exciting—those types of things you hopefully get a little better at. We're definitely more conscious of how to make a song grow and change through

its course. Like at the beginning of "Goodbye Hooray," I'm playing along with Flea and catching the accents, but I'm not playing too much yet—you have to *build* it to make it exciting. By the last chorus, I didn't know that Josh was going to be going [sings squealing guitar sounds], but I knew this was the time to go for it with some fills.

MD: The thing that is always obvious, despite how the songs are built up and overdubbed, is that you guys are a *band*. You get to play.

Chad: And that's very rewarding. It has to be done right, but the nature of this group is that there's interaction, and I'm proud of the way that we do have a sound, no matter what types of things we do. We have a "thing"—it's a performance.

MD: The collaborative nature of the band might be one reason why you've sustained several changes in the lead guitar spot over the years.

Chad: Yeah, and I find that a non-drummer's suggestions will often spark my ideas. Flea, for example, knows that my immediate go-to thing is hi-hat/kick/snare. Not all the time, but unless it sounds like it should be more tribal, I start out with a traditional rock beat. I try to come up with something cool, but that's my go-to thing. And sometimes we'll be jamming, and he'll be like, Try something like this on the toms [sings something complex and crazed] I'm not going to try to exactly replicate how he sang it. Instead I try to do my own version of it. So it's still my thing, but I wouldn't have thought of that initial idea. And lots of times it ends up being really cool and different.

Being open to ideas is very important because it challenges you, and you can grow from that. The song is king. We all have the same goal. You never know—that weird tom thing might inspire Josh to play something else on guitar, which makes the rhythm change and makes Anthony's vocal cadence change. It could have this domino effect, all because someone suggested a tom part. And that's the beauty and fun of the creative process. It doesn't always work, but you have to be open.

MD: As much as the Chili Peppers are your baby, your playing with the Meatbats and Chickenfoot somehow seems almost more in line with your personality. You really get your ya-yas out in a very *rock* way in those situations.

Chad: I think you're right. Chickenfoot is like that music I grew up with, that classic rock, Deep Purple, jammy thing. I don't write with them for six months or a year, and I don't go on tour for eighteen months with those guys. We

Ash Newell

get together for a short amount of time and have this energy spurt, and it's really fun. But it's a different thing. I get my inner Paice on—not my inner peace, my inner Paice, if you will. [laughs] It's like I'm fourteen, and I'm playing with Sammy Hagar from Montrose and Mike Anthony and Joe Satriani.

But I think that if I was doing that all the time…it's not that it's limiting, but there's this certain thing that we do really well. In the Chili Peppers, one of the reasons I think we've been able to stay relevant and have a long career is that we're not afraid to try anything, and whatever it is that we're trying to do, as long as it's a good song, it sounds like us. And we're not trying to not sound like us; we're just taking what's given to us by the musical gods and working on it to make it good. And that's something I'm very proud of. It's always a new thing. We don't write on the road; we write the music that reflects where we're at as people and as players in the band, at that time, and people are getting a snapshot of that.

When we were doing our *Greatest Hits* record in 2003, Warner Brothers wanted a couple extra songs. So we went in to write a couple during the next break on the tour we were on at the time, and we recorded like sixteen songs. They weren't all great, but twelve of them were probably good. So we put the *Greatest Hits* album out and toured a little bit more, and then we were going to come back and write some more songs, and I was like, "Let's just write another ten, take maybe seven out of that, add it to the others we'd previously done, and we'll have a record."

I remember John Frusciante was like, "Hmm…that was like nine months ago; I'm not really doing the arpeggiated thing anymore. I'm playing differently, I'm listening to different stuff, so I'm going to write different music." So there's an album that we did that I don't know if anyone's ever going to hear. But we're pretty true to that

Ash Newell

idea of recording what we're into at the time. And that's what's exciting to me—showing up at practice and wondering, What's going to happen today?

MD: You're involved in three distinct bands, with some strong personalities.

Chad: Yeah, in Chickenfoot Sammy's real vocal, like, "This is the greatest song ever!"[laughs] Joe's sense of humor is more subtle, and Mike's probably the most easygoing. I'm the off-the-wall guy, and they embrace that energy.

In the Chili Peppers I'm not really like that. It's more about being the real solid foundation, the heart, the engine, very reliable. I'm going to come up with something solid and it's going to make the guys feel good, be the right tempo for Anthony to sing over. I really want to be supportive, though even after all these years, sometimes that leads to me not speaking out, whereas in other situations I might. You've got Flea, who's this really strong musical personality coming in with all of these ideas, and Anthony has lots of ideas about what he likes. And Josh is starting to come into his own in the group. At first he was a little timid, understandably. I feel like I'm kind of the connection between everybody. It's just a different dynamic. I'm not a different person, but you read situations differently.

MD: What you play is very different in those situations as well.

Chad: Yeah, sonically, in terms of parts… The only thing that's probably the same is my feel. But the music is different, the sound is different, and obviously the musicians play differently. The Chili Peppers are tighter, more part oriented, and maybe that comes from playing together so long and having a very part-conscious producer.

MD: What about the Meatbats?

Chad: That's a free-for-all. [laughs] It's a band with a sense of humor, and we play instrumental music that's kooky. I think instrumental music gets pigeonholed as serious, only for musicians— this muso, shreddy, noodly, look-at-me thing. The Meatbats songs have strong structures and verses and choruses, and there's no singing, so I get to stretch out a little. We're not competing with the Lady Gagas of the world. We're in a very niche market. But it's music that we really like.

MD: Watching the Meatbats at the winter NAMM show and at the Iridium in NYC, what struck me was that it's a perfect live band. Did you have something specific in mind when you started the group?

Chad: There were no specific ideas—there aren't a lot of thought-out ideas to most of what I do. [laughs] But we do enjoy playing with each other, and obviously I wouldn't be doing it if it wasn't really fun. And I get to really…overplay.

MD: Which seems appropriate—you appropriately overplay.

Ash Newell

Chad: Right! In instrumental rock, yes, you are allowed to appropriately overplay. There's a lot of room for improvising within the structures of the songs, everyone's a good listener, and there's dynamics. We want people to have a good time. I don't go out and see a ton of instrumental music, but when I do, a lot of the time it sounds kind of self-indulgent. It can be a serious, clap-between-the-solos thing, but we're not that. So I think sometimes people are taken aback by our, uh…

MD: Your bawdiness?

Chad: Yeah—and then I have a microphone, and that's not good. [laughs]

MD: Well, they should know what they're getting. It's called Chad Smith's Bombastic Meatbats, after all.

Chad: That's the thing, right from the name on down.

MD: About the improv aspect, what's your approach? When those moments come up when there's an opportunity to…

Chad: …to go for it?

MD: Yeah. How planned out is that? How far ahead are you thinking? Do you have a bag of tricks that you pull from?

Chad: If I do *any* of those things, I'm screwed. [laughs] Thinking, me, on the gig? Bad. Plan stuff out? Not really a good idea. And you know, I think I sort of tried to do that when we filmed a show at the Iridium, and it ended up sounding…planned out. It wasn't good. In any musical situation, certainly with the Bats, if I'm thinking, *Here comes that section*, I'm not in the moment anymore when your pure self comes through.

Regarding a bag of tricks, I don't have one. If I do, it's very small, and it doesn't have much in it!

MD: How about communication on stage?

Chad: We have signposts, cues for each other. Like, I do this thing that sets up that other thing, or I'm going to play something and then we'll do it in unison.

Peter Erskine once wrote that when you're having a musical conversation with someone, you don't repeat what they say, like, "Hey, that was really good," "Hey, that was really good." It should be more like, "Hey, that was really good." "Oh, thanks a lot." "Sure, hey, maybe try this." "Oh, I hear what you're saying." For a long time, I thought what was cool was repeating what a musician just played, like, "Look how clever I am, what a good listener I am. Look how fast I got on that."

MD: Repetition is the first thing you think of.

Chad: Exactly. It takes more of an evolved musical palette to respond in a unique way that doesn't sound random. And maybe that's where the bag of tricks comes in—having things that I can do technically to express myself. When I do clinics and master classes, I say that you should get your hands and rudiments together so that when you play, you have a way to express yourself through your feet and hands. I can't do everything I want to do in the moment—I'm not good enough. But I can do this, and I can say what I want to say pretty well.

MD: There's so much smiling on stage with the Meatbats.

Chad: For a jazz gig, I guess there is. [laughs]

MD: That's a big thing, though.

Chad: It is, it is! First of all, you've got to enjoy the people you're working with. And when you're having a good musical conversation, there's humor, there's quiet parts, introspective parts. For me that's kind of a normal extension of your feelings. And we're doing it in front of a crowd. I mean, I can be kind of a hambone at times, but that's not a put-on. It's me—for better or worse!

MD: You've said that the Meatbats are not your band, despite your name being in front.

Chad: The record label was like, "You're in a popular group—if you don't mind, it wouldn't be a bad idea to put your name on it." And the other guys were okay with it, and I was like, "Well, uh, okay, I guess." I don't know how I ended up on the mic. I suppose I'm a little bit of a stronger personality than the other guys when it comes to talking. In Chickenfoot, Sam and I go back and forth. Joe doesn't talk, and that's just him—the glasses and bald head and science fiction thing, a very thoughtful musician. Mike talks a little bit, but you can never understand what he's saying, his voice is so high. [laughs] But Sam needed a foil, and that's the way our personalities are in the group. That's how we were together when we first met in Mexico—we're friends.

Ash Newell

MD: Chickenfoot's got a brand-new second album coming out, but because of the Chili Peppers tour starting up, you're not going on the road with them, right?

Chad: Yeah, they'll have to get somebody else to do it. It's always been, like, I'm in this other band—the housekeepers, as I like to call them. [laughs]

MD: With all these groups being active, it's been great for your drumming. You're playing a lot, especially with the Meatbats and Chickenfoot.

Chad: Yeah, playing a lot—and often. Appropriately overplaying...yeah, I like that!

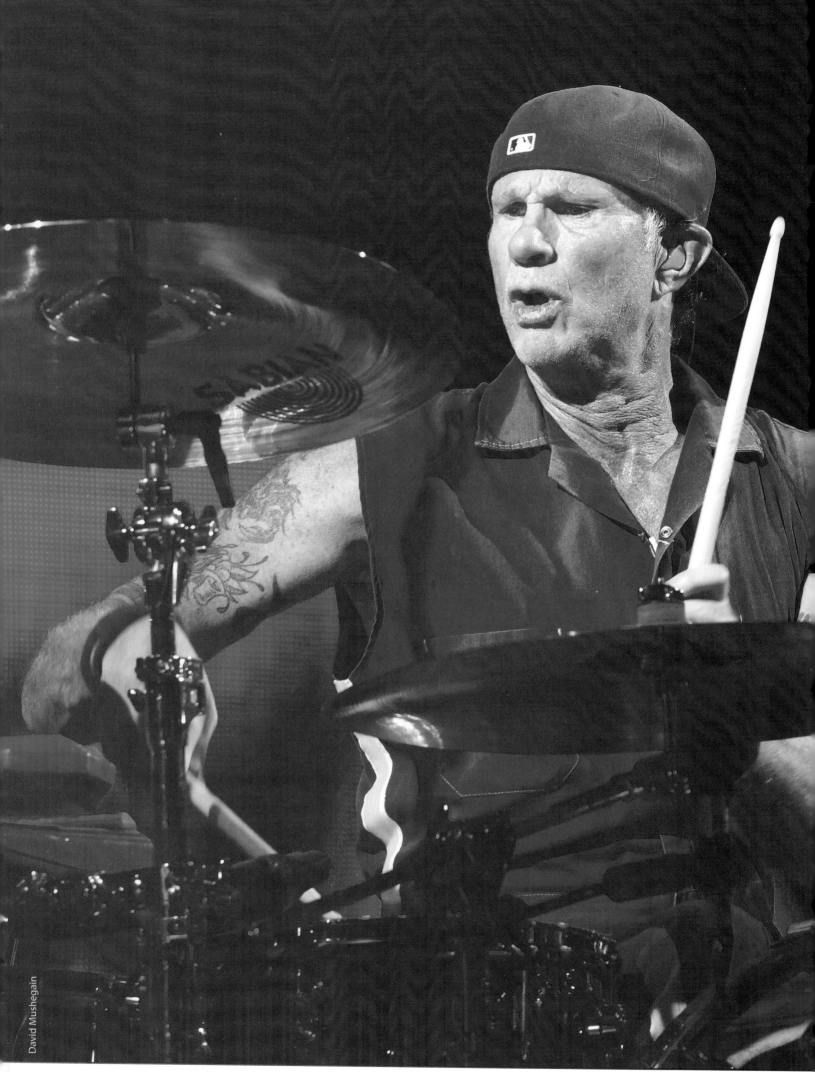

David Mushegain

No Ordinary Man

The October 2020 Interview

by David Ciauro

The longtime Red Hot Chili Peppers drummer is enjoying a wave of great reviews for his work on the new, critically acclaimed Ozzy Osbourne album, *Ordinary Man*. The takeaway? If there's one contemporary drummer on the planet who wholly embodies the heart and soul of classic-rock drumming, it must surely be him.

Strange times these are, indeed. On Tuesday, May 12, I received a request to conduct an interview with Chad Smith for an *MD* cover story. Of course, my first instinct was to say, "Yes!" But in an era when second-guessing everything is the new normal, my immediate next thought was, "But what are we going to talk about?"

It's true that the Red Hot Chili Peppers had made headlines at the tail end of 2019 when they welcomed back guitarist John Frusciante, who initially joined the band around the same time Chad did back in 1988. But with all the current uncertainty surrounding Covid-19, what did the future look like for the reunion? Chad should have been on tour somewhere in Spain when we spoke in June, but instead he was at home with some free time before he had to pick up his kids from their last day of school, and then do the kind of drive-by goodbye celebration that's become commonplace in most neighborhoods.

While coronavirus may have delayed Chili Peppers activities, it didn't come in time to derail the release of Ozzy Osbourne's critically acclaimed new release, *Ordinary Man*, which Chad, along with guitarist/producer Andrew Watt and Guns N' Roses bassist Duff McKagan, had written and recorded all the material for in just four days. Listening to Chad tear through the album's eleven tracks, it's immediately apparent that he's completely in his element driving the music of one of classic rock's most iconic voices. The drummer might be known as the ultimate punk-funkster of the Woodstock II generation, but *Ordinary Man* is perhaps the purest example to date of his ability to tap right into the music that formed his playing aesthetic from day one: the brawny, boiling heavy rock of the '70s, when the only thing bigger than the riffs were the personalities of the players laying them down. Clearly Chad Smith can hang with rock giants from that or any generation.

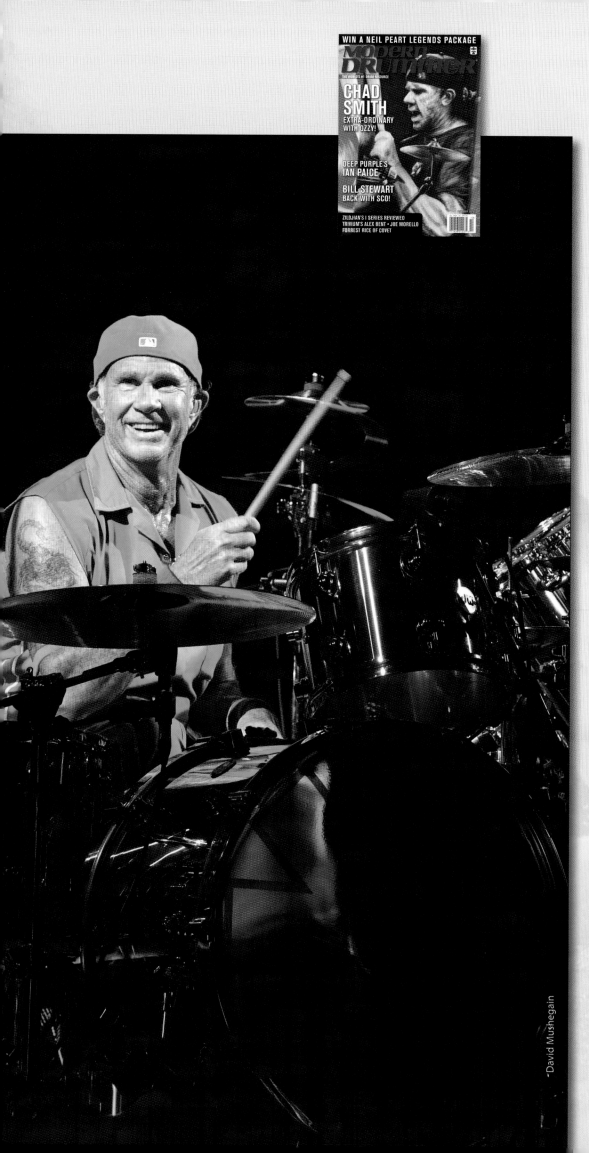

•David Mushegain

MD: I'd like to start this interview talking about your recent Instagram posts, where you posted a different iconic drum groove each day. Those videos put the nail in the casket of the idea that the sound of a drummer comes from a drum. You definitely were not playing the *Blood Sugar Sex Magik* snare drum that everybody knows, it was cell-phone audio with no mics on the kit, and I didn't get the impression you painstakingly mixed anything in post. Yet you weren't holding back hitting the drums in this big open space, and no matter what groove you played, the sound was so identifiably *you*. It proved that it always has been, and always will be, about the drummer, not the drum.

Chad: Wow, I never thought of it like that, but yeah. That kit is an old mid-'60s Slingerland. When I was a kid, the first kit I had was a gold sparkle Slingerland that I'd subsequently sold for a bag of weed in high school. So I bought a similar kit for nostalgia that I keep set up in my living room. That room has high ceilings and wood floors, and it sounds really loud but beautiful. The compression on the phone audio does help things pop, but I wasn't thinking about anything other than going back to when I was in high school and playing grooves I used to play along to, like the Beatles, Stones, Sabbath, and Zeppelin. I grew up on those songs, and it was just fun to do.

But David, you're right, if you have the same drumset, the same song, and seven different drummers playing, it will always sound different. It's all in the touch, it's all in your hands and your feet and your coordination, how you feel the music, and how your limbs are placed, and that's why everybody sounds different. That's a beautiful thing!

MD: I attended the Bonzo Bash back in 2013 while at NAMM, and that served as the perfect case study in what you're talking about. The kit remained the same with a revolving door of drummers playing Zeppelin tunes, and it was very clear who spent their time playing in bands or with other musicians as opposed to those who approached the drums as a solo instrument. There's certainly value in both, but from an audience's perspective, it was obvious who grooved *with* the band, because heads were bobbing or they weren't. Knowing your history, you are definitely in the former camp,

with other people. It's the human interaction that I feel is missing in our youth culture today, because everything is so insular. It's great to play in a room and record yourself. But as a musician, especially a drummer playing rock 'n' roll music… drums really aren't used as a melodic instrument. You're part of the rhythm section, and you're the timekeeper—you need to play with other people! To me, to truly be playing *music* you have to be playing with other people. That's the fun part, the human connection, being in a band with other people. That's the give and take, and where you learn to listen. To me, that's making music. Playing by myself was always a means to be able to play with other people. That's what I love to do.

David Mushegain

so do you feel there would be a Chad Smith if you spent a greater majority or your time woodshedding rather than playing with other musicians?

Chad: That's a great question, and I think that's a really important thing. You do need to practice to develop your technique and have your chops so you can play with other people. When I think back to when I was growing up, drumming along to all my records in a basement in Detroit, I approached it so that I tried to feel like I was in the band. Sure, I was playing by myself, but that was my version of playing with other people until I actually started playing

MD: Being in a band where the human connection is so obvious, and groove is something that is more about a feel in the moment rather than gridded precision, what are your thoughts on how recording technology has impacted the concept of what it means to be a good timekeeper?

Chad: It's natural for music to live and breathe. It's natural for tempos to pick up going into the chorus and settle back down into the verse. That's a normal human thing that happens when you're playing with other people, and there's no substitute for that. Now, yes, there's a lot of recorded music being done to some form of click track or beat map,

and that's become the norm, and that works for certain kinds of music. But call me old-fashioned, but the Chili Peppers, we just play! And the reality is that now, a lot of people just can't do it. People have become so reliant on editing and the modern conveniences of recording technology, but I always ask, "What about the performance of the song?" And that's what's missing. It may sound "perfect," but it's missing the emotion, and that emotion is what connects with people. Sometimes the pursuit of trying to make something sound perfect by taking out all the little mistakes, or little pushes and pulls, maybe they don't realize that those imperfections are the thing that make a song great. I saw somebody on YouTube quantizing Bonham's drumming to demonstrate this point.

MD: That was Rick Beato. That video is a great example of what you're talking about.

Chad: Yeah, a perfect example! I way prefer the human element, and that's not to say being able to have control over the click and accurately play ahead of or behind it isn't a great skill to have. But if you have a band that can play, f'in play!

MD: Those editing tricks may make the mixing easier, but certainly haven't afforded us the next wave of great rock bands.

Chad: It doesn't make better music. It's actually detrimental. Because as a musician you had to commit to what you were playing when you were recording to tape.

MD: So that commitment has waned with the luxury of being able to comp ad nauseum.

Chad: Most new engineers don't have a clue how to cut tape or have ever recorded with a tape machine. We've done all our records to tape, up until *The Getaway*.

MD: How hard is it to find studios now that still do offer the option to record to tape?

Chad: I mean, you're going to have to ask for it. Some people swear by the sound of analog, the saturation, the little bit of distortion in the low end. But in all honesty, with how far the technology has come and all the plug-ins and different stuff that I don't really know about, it's sonically really close. I think back when we recorded *Stadium Arcadium*, we recorded both to tape and Pro Tools and then did the Pepsi challenge: "Which one do you think is tape; which one do you think is digital?" And it was really hard to tell—we were just guessing. Most importantly, a good song needs to be the primary source. Follow that with other good source materials like a nice-sounding room, good instruments, good mics, good musicians, good outboard gear, and the difference between analog and digital can be really difficult to discern.

I did a track on Halsey's latest record that was produced by Greg Kurstin, and he recorded my drums to tape—just the drums—and then dumped that into Pro Tools. That was the first time I had recorded to tape in a long time.

MD: You've appeared on a good number of records from artists other than your main bands. Have you continued doing that in recent times?

Chad: I've played on other people's stuff in the past, not tons of stuff, and mostly it was through [Chili Peppers producer] Rick Rubin, who I've obviously had a long history with. Back in the early '90s I got to play on a Johnny Cash record, Dixie Chicks, and some others that were uncredited. Usually it was artists that didn't have bands.

In the last couple years I've been working a lot with Andrew Watt, who produced Ozzy's record. I've done tracks for Post Malone, Sam Smith, Jake Bugg, Dua Lipa, Charlie Puth, Miley Cyrus, and Lana Del Rey, all with Andrew. He's a hot pop producer, but he's a rock dude. The pop world is pretty small, and once he had a hit with that Camila Cabello song "Havana," he was in demand. We're good buddies, so any time he needed a drummer, he'd give me a call, and that's how this Ozzy thing started. It was a song for Post's record. Post mentioned how much he loved Ozzy, and Andrew knew Kelly Osbourne, who was familiar with Post's music. Of course, Ozzy had no clue at first of who Post was, but it was great working on that song.

Ozzy was amazing to be around—so funny and so sweet, and he did not disappoint. He was peeing in the planters and telling fart jokes; it was just so awesome. There's only one Prince of Darkness, and I was just trying not to be a dork around him. But he was really frail because, unbeknownst to us, he had fallen and hurt his neck a year ago and was doing rehab and just not getting better. The bulletproof Ozzy wasn't getting better, so he had been pretty bummed. After we were done and Ozzy left, Kelly was almost in tears saying how she hadn't seen him that happy in six months, and how being creative and making music is what he really loves to do. So we were like, shit, let's write songs for Ozzy! We needed a great bass player, because Andrew is a great guitarist. I'd played with Duff McKagan a week earlier at a

David Mushegain

Chad's Live Setup

Drums: DW Collector's series stainless steel kit
• 6.5x14 Collector's series heavy gauge steel snare with die-cast hoops
• 6.5x13 stainless steel auxiliary snare
• 9x12 tom
• 12x14 floor tom
• 14x16 floor tom
• 16x24 bass drum
• 6" Rata Toms (cluster of 4)
• 10" Remo Rototom
• 29" vintage Rogers timpani

Cymbals: Sabian (all in brilliant finish)
• 20" Sprymbal (spiral cymbal)
• 11" AAX X-Plosion splash
• 15" AAX X-Celerator hi-hats
• 19" AA Rock crash
• 21" AA Rock ride
• 20" AA Rock crash
• 21" AA Medium crash
• 21" AA Holy China
• 10" stack: AA Mini Holy China/AAX Aero splash

Percussion: LP Chad Smith Ridge Rider cowbell and medium Jam Block

Hardware: DW 9000 series stands and 5000 series bass drum pedal

Heads: Remo Controlled Sound X Coated snare batter and Ambassador snare-side, Controlled Sound Clear aux snare batter and Ambassador snare-side, Smooth White Emperor tom batters and Ambassador Clear resonants, Powerstroke P4 Clear bass drum batter and Ambassador front, Controlled Sound Clear Rata Tom batters

Sticks: Vater Chad Smith's Funk Blaster stick, T1 Ultra Staccato timpani mallet

Accessories: Vater stick bag, JH Audio JH/16v2 Pro in-ear monitors

charity event in Montana, so I called him up. He was in town and he was saying that the band wasn't doing anything at the moment, and I said, "Wanna write and record some songs for Ozzy?" Of course he said yes. Nobody says no to Ozzy! Everyone showed up for this: Elton John, Tom Morello, Slash, Post Malone. It was a perfect storm of everybody's schedule being aligned and timing working out.

Andrew, Duff, and I went to Andrew's studio in the basement of his house and thought, well, what's our favorite Ozzy and Sabbath stuff? What would a modern cool Ozzy album sound like? We all collaborated and wrote and recorded twelve songs in four afternoons, banging out three songs a day from scratch. We'd finish a tune and cut it right away, tracking the performance all the way through. We didn't chop it up in post or anything, like we were talking about earlier. We were so energized by the idea of writing a great record for Ozzy, because with everything that he'd experienced, who knew if it would be his last. A lot of Ozzy's lyrics on this album were reflective about life and death. It's heavy, but it was so much fun and it turned out great, and Ozzy loved it. No one sounds like him. That instrument, the voice, is the most beautiful instrument because it's so unique. The emotion in a voice is something that Pro Tools

can't do for you. Fourteen-year-old Chad was pinching himself through that whole experience!

MD: I remember watching an interview with Ozzy years ago where he said that he still hasn't put out his *White Album*. This album definitely felt like it could be that album.

Chad: Ozzy *loves* the Beatles! He was really pleased with the way it came out, and people seem to like it. And this wasn't even a labor of love for me, it was really an honor to be able to write music and play with Ozzy.

MD: Listening to the record, there are noticeable shifts in drum tone, especially the snare drum from song to song. Were specific tones discussed before you tracked?

Chad: No, that would all be in the mix. There's no samples or sound replacements, and I didn't swap out drums. It's all on the same kit. Maybe [we used] a different snare or intentionally deeper tuning on the ballad "Ordinary Man" with Elton John. In all honesty, the tone probably did change slightly because we were tracking three songs a day and I was beating the crap out of the snare, and then I would change the snare head, so you are probably hearing a slight change from song to song.

MD: Going back to what we were talking about earlier and the importance of playing with other people, now with

David Mushegain

David Mushegain

the quarantine, when was the last time you jammed with anybody?

Chad: Well, I'm not going to be a namedropper [laughs], but some of my neighbors are in bands that everybody knows, and we jammed in the backyard of one of our neighbors that is a very well-known actor. But the Chili Peppers are back to writing a few days a week. It's just the four of us in a room with nobody else around.

MD: And John's back in the band.

Chad: Yep, John's back in the band. We were supposed to be on tour in Spain right now, but since touring looks to be postponed until next year, we started writing and are hoping to make a record.

MD: You all live close enough where jamming in person is a reality?

Chad: Yeah, we're not rehearsing virtually.

MD: Is there a noticeable shift in tone that's organically coming out because this is being written in such an interesting time?

Chad: It's all in there, everything you're experiencing as a person—we're all products of our surroundings. It's impossible for it not to affect the music, but it's not doom-and-gloom or music for the end of the world. If anything, we're writing uplifting, positive songs. There's nothing that's ever been preconceived; we're always writing about what we feel. But what's currently going on is heavy! Last night I was driving home at 10 o'clock. I was in the Beverly Hills area, and until I got to the freeway, which was like five or six miles, I saw like five cars—in L.A.! It was weird.

MD: Is there a more positive charge or enhanced appreciation of being able to connect with your musical brethren right now?

Chad: Yes, and having John come back into our group is a new shot of energy. We've been in and out of each other's lives since 1988, and it's been ten years since we played with John, but during that time we all continued to grow as people and as musicians. So it's new but it's still familiar. He's changed as a person and as a musician, too, and it's going to be different, but at the same time, for whatever reason, we do have this *thing* when we play together that we sound like us. No matter how fast, slow, or hard we play, that's still there, which is pretty cool! It's exciting to wake up knowing we don't have anything, but that probably by 3 o'clock we're going to have something that we didn't have before. That's the greatest feeling as a creative person, and I'm grateful for having the ability with these three other people that I love to make music with. Sometimes it's great, and sometimes it's not so great, but there will be something new that didn't exist before, and I *love* that. That, and a little bit of coffee, is what gets me up in the morning.

MD: Do you know who's going to produce the new record?

Chad: We've been talking to Rick Rubin, and he's excited about us recording and we have a real history with him, so that would be the obvious choice, but we're still early on in this process, so no formal decisions have been made.

MD: You mentioned how when the four of you play, for whatever reason, you sound the way you sound, and it's a sound that is immediately identifiable. The drummers we all seem to care the most about are the ones with this certain intangible quality that we call "their sound." You fall into that category, but for you, what do you love about the drummers that have influenced you?

Chad: That's what makes the drummer unique. The person behind the sound. What does this drummer have that sets them apart? I was always taken with guys who had identifiable sounds, like Phil Collins, Stewart Copeland, Bonham, Ringo, Charlie Watts, Keith Moon, and Neil Peart. You hear them and you know it's them. Take Neil Peart. I've been lucky enough to meet and spend some time with him, and you get to know a little about his personality and the way he thought, how meticulous and detail oriented he was, how smart he was, his dry sense of humor—you hear all of that in his drumming. For all the drummers we love, their drumming is truly an extension of their personality.

I like to play loud, and it's just the way I choose to express myself. I like the power, but I also know when it's time not to be loud. That's real, and that's what people connect with—authenticity. So for me, reading about other drummers, once in a while I'd be curious to know how they got a certain sound or whatever, but mostly I wanted to know why they played the way they played. I wanted insight into their personality and experiences and influences that informed how they approached the drums and how they think about music. I think Ian Paice said this about Ringo. People sometimes like to poo-poo Ringo, but Ian said the one thing you can say about every Beatles song is that they all feel great; that's what you want, and that's why Ringo is a legend. And that goes into the whole discussion about "What is feel?" and "What is pocket?"

MD: The feel of a band and what makes a song feel good are often more about a connection between the musicians playing together than the actual drum part that's "fueling" the groove.

Chad: Andrew and I were listening to an isolated drum part by an iconic drummer recently. There are a bunch of these isolated tracks available now to listen to on YouTube, and we were listening to this track and were taken aback at how unimpressive it was in isolation. If someone posted it as their own playing, it would be torn apart, but when you put it back into the mix and give it context, all of a sudden it was magic! Where you are in the pocket really depends on the other people you're playing with—that creates the pocket!

But everyone's different, and there's a real difference between a drummer or musician in a band that has a unique sound and their own definition of a pocket compared to a session drummer or musician that has to know how to identify the perfect feel for that given song.

MD: From the videos I've seen of you in a clinic setting, it seems that when you're playing solo, you're accompanying some music or beat in your head, which helps you find the pocket.

Chad: The therapist in you is coming out! "Tell me more about the sounds in your head, Chad!" [laughs] Well, those things are weird for me, because I am in a band and that's really my thing more than playing solos. I can do it, but it's not my thing. Other guys are masters at the clinic and educational side of drumming. I play in a band. I have some technique and I can showcase it, but going back to what we started talking about, I prefer playing with other people, even if they're in my head! [laughs] But everything to me should be musical, so when it's just the drums and a rhythmic thing and I'm not a jazz drummer playing melodies on the toms—though I wish I was that good—it's more about thinking about the feel I'm trying to convey. So if I'm playing a James Brown type of groove or a Bonham-style groove, I'll often think about an exit strategy of where I can go from here that gives me sign posts to follow when playing in a solo environment.

When I was fourteen or fifteen, I went to a clinic in Ann Arbor, Michigan, by one of my favorite drummers at the

WIN A NEIL PEART LEGENDS PACKAGE

MODERN DRUMMER
THE WORLD'S #1 DRUM RESOURCE

CHAD SMITH
EXTRA-ORDINARY WITH OZZY!

DEEP PURPLE'S
IAN PAICE

BILL STEWART
BACK WITH SCO!

ZILDJIAN'S I SERIES REVIEWED
TRIVIUM'S ALEX BENT • JOE MORELLO
FORREST RICE OF COVET

David Mushegain

time. He walked onstage, didn't acknowledge the audience, and proceeded to play a mind-blowing twenty-minute solo. Then he came to the front of the stage, grabbed a mic, and said, "Any questions?" Clearly he didn't seem to be in a good mood, and it was so intimidating and polarizing—you either wanted to quit playing or it inspired you to practice twenty-five hours a day. I had rock star ambitions at that age, and I remember thinking, if I ever do a clinic, I'm going to be nice and open and engaging. What I love about the drumming community is how sharing they are with each other. So when I do clinics, I'll play along to some Chili Peppers tunes and do a little solo, but then I'll talk to the audience and let them know I'm human and I'm glad to share anything. I'm an open book! If you want to talk about drums and music, I'll tell you whatever my experience has been. If it can help you or even help you reconsider some things, the important thing is to learn from your experiences.

People like Dom Famularo and Terry Bozzio are made for the clinic scene; that's a whole other level. But for me, if I can

inspire a kid to play the drums, then it's a success. I try to put myself in the shoes of having the opportunity to see Mitch Mitchell or John Bonham at a clinic up close and personal when I was a kid and being able to ask them a question; I am 100 percent there for that.

MD: That speaks volumes about the age-old argument of who is the best drummer. For me, the best drummers have always been the ones that inspired people to pick up the sticks, and that's incredibly personal and subjective.

Chad: Right on! By no means do you have to be in a famous band, but that helps only because of the number of people that are exposed to your music. If someone watches the Chili Peppers play, sees me, and thinks, "That guy looks like he's having a blast. I want to do *that*," that's the best! When Ringo was on *Ed Sullivan* and exposed to millions of viewers, that inspired a generation of drummers. Then after that, it's up to you to do something with that inspiration.

MD: I think we're all waiting for that next rock band to inspire future generations. Because that's the thing about the great bands—it wasn't just a great drummer. For every Chili Peppers fan that picked up a pair of sticks for the first time because of you, there were an equal number of people that picked up a bass or guitar because of Flea and John.

Chad: One silver lining of this quarantine is that people are starting to play instruments again. There are all different levels of playing an instrument and pursuing your identity as a musician, but you have to be okay with whatever path you choose. If it's recreational or a hobby, great! If it's to pursue a career, is it to be in a band, or to be a studio musician, or be in a pit band on Broadway? Whatever it is, you have to commit to it. If you're going to pursue it as a career, be sure you have the drive to see it through.

MD: It seems that it's especially important for kids to understand how much work it is, that the glamorous aspects are just the tip of the iceberg. The two hours onstage in front of an audience are supported by hours in cramped quarters traveling between venues, being away from home for 200-plus days a year, press junkets answering the same questions day after day, and the stress of having to write and record an album that resonates with your audience.

Chad: And that's if you're ever lucky enough to get to that point and gain a following. But that's really what weeds out the people that are more interested in the perceived lifestyle than the livelihood. Because it truly is hard work. There are no shortcuts to this career.

Tony Woolliscroft

Tony Woolliscroft

Tony Woollscroft

Tony Woolliscroft

Tony Woolliscroft

The Music

by Terry Branam

Chad Smith is one of the most recognizable drummers in modern music. His hard-hitting funk/rock style has been the driving force behind the iconic band Red Hot Chili Peppers for decades. Whether laying down the funk alongside his rhythm section counterpart Flea or igniting his formidable chops to push an extended jam to the outer limits, Smith always has a sense of style and confidence in his performances. Chad's sound is an extension of his personality and is permanently cemented into the spirit of rock and roll. His drumming is an influence on generations of drummers.

Chad's drumming style is the perfect mix of funk attitude, rock and roll swagger, and song-based sensitivity. His agile right foot thumps in harmony with Flea's signature bass style to create a colossal pocket. He is a champion of ghost notes, as they provide the glue to his kick and snare designs. Chad's penchant for playing the right thing at the right time is always the centerpiece of his musical statements.

Smith's colossal sound stems from his relaxed, flowing technique. His wrists and arms make big arching motions as they move around the kit, while his legs bounce up and down on the pedals in time with the song. He commits his entire body to the groove. Chad's signature cracking snare tone—mixed with his dynamic hi-hat approach—excites the upper frequencies. The low end and midrange are filled in with a deep, punchy kick drum and throaty toms. He balances the kit's voices like a mixing engineer, bringing certain elements forward when the song calls for it and pushing others back. Smith's dedication to the pocket is significant, and his mark on drumming is illustrious.

What follows is just a sampling of the incredible music Chad Smith has made since first debuting with the Chili Peppers on *Mother's Milk* in 1989.

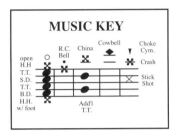

"Salute to Kareem," *Mother's Milk*

The instrumental ditty "Salute to Kareem" features Chad's hard-hitting pocket. He complements Flea's aggressive bassline with a syncopated James Brown-style beat. The snare drum displaces to the "and" of beat 4 on the first bar of the two-measure pattern. (0:00)

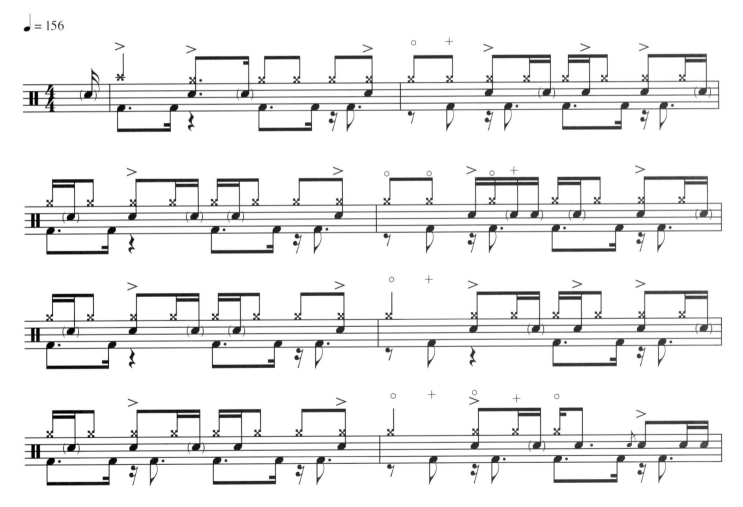

Chad takes a funky solo later in the song. This is an excellent example of how he can keep the groove locked in while displaying some impressive chops. (2:10)

The Music

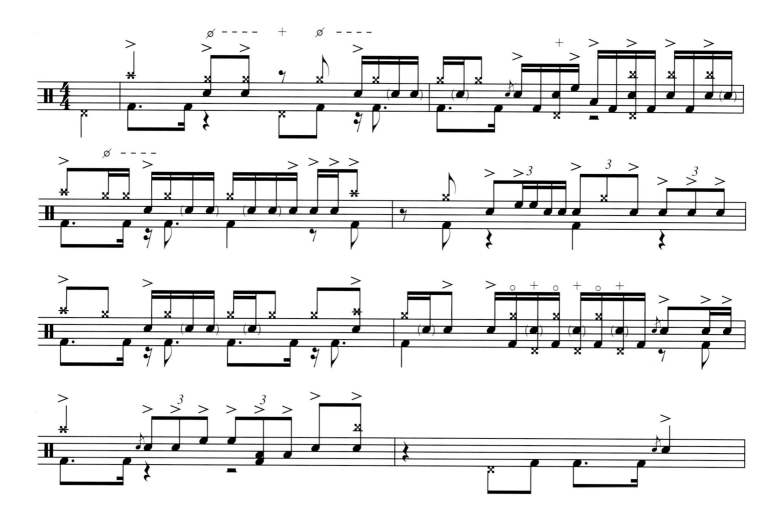

"Suck my Kiss," *Blood Sugar Sex Magik*

It's difficult not to nod your head to the slamming beat of "Suck my Kiss." Chad's kick drum teams up with the guitar and bass parts in the intro. The hi-hat punctuates the upbeat accents—a tip of the hat to the great R&B drummer Bernard Purdie. (0:04)

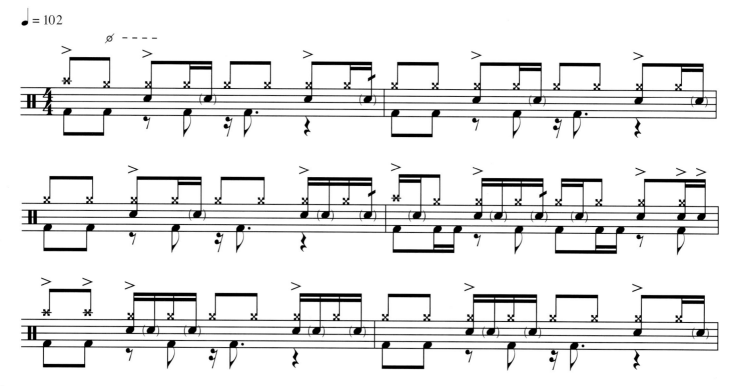

A quick sextuplet fill sets up the unison accent on the "and" of beat 2 leading into the chorus. The drum groove twists on the second half of the first measure to work with the rhythm section's riff. (1:03)

The Music

"Breaking the Girl," *Blood Sugar Sex Magik*

Chad pays homage to Mitch Mitchell's legendary "Manic Depression" groove with the rolling triplet feel of "Breaking the Girl." He integrates descending triplets at the end of the measure to add momentum. (0:49)

Metallic percussion accompanies the powerful bridge groove. Chad plays strong accents on the snare and toms at the end of the two-measure phrase. (3:00)

"Warped," *One Hot Minute*

Smith's playing on the rocked-out "Warped" pushes the band with a scrappy beat that pops the second snare drum hit to the "and" of beat 4. His right hand moves up and down the ride cymbal, mixing it up with the bell. (0:46)

The big fills in the B section play around the guitar accents. (1:24)

Chad lays down a Bo Diddley–type of tom beat under the guitar solo. (2:33)

The Music

He cleverly catches the band's accented hits before the last verse. (3:05)

The whole kit is employed in the rowdy outro. Chad smacks the immense accents on the snare and China while playing an alternating pattern with the feet. The interplay between the floor tom and the bass drum resembles a 16th-note double bass groove. (4:01)

♩ = 66

slight rit.

"By the Way," *By the Way*

The mellow intro of "By the Way" has Chad playing a tasteful sidestick groove on all four quarter notes. He plays open hi-hat quarter notes at the end of the phrase to accentuate Flea's bass line. (0:16)

The band kicks into high gear before the verse, and Chad comes in with a strong tom/snare beat. He drops in controlled ghost notes on the snare after the backbeats to keep the 16ths flowing. (0:33)

The Music

Chad drops in some left-hand drags on the chorus groove that add weight to the bass drum part. A catchy four-stroke ruff neatly wraps up the phrase. (1:02)

"Readymade," *Stadium Arcadium*

There is a clever displacement in the main riff of "Readymade." Smith turns the beat around by pushing the pattern an 8th note backward on the second measure and then snapping it back into place at the end of the fourth measure. (0:11)

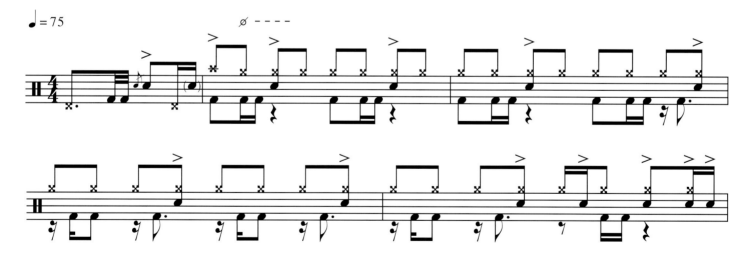

The hi-hat and cowbell toggle back and forth on the chorus. Chad's open hi-hat adds a cushion under the legato background vocals, while the chunky cowbell beat sets off the heavy rhythm-section riff. (1:03)

Chad lays down a greasy 16th-note pocket in the bridge. Distorted overdubbed percussion adds a unique texture to the groove. (2:59)

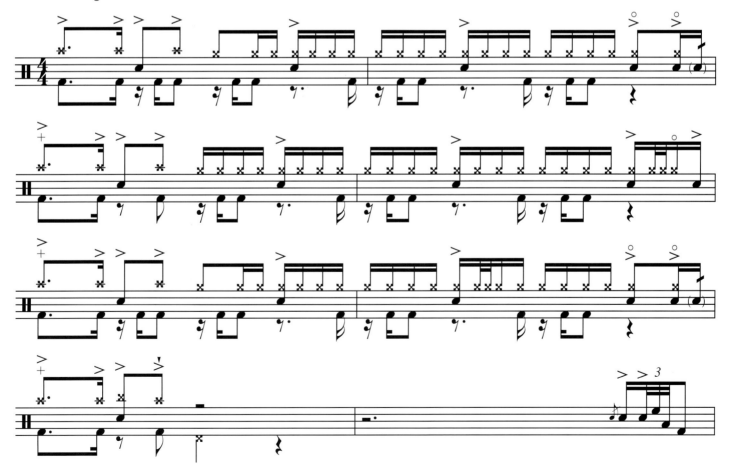

The Music

"Charlie," *Stadium Arcadium*

"Charlie" has a funky James Brown-inspired feel in the verse with Chad's signature ghost notes and a displaced backbeat on the "and" of beat 4. His lively hi-hat playing adds lots of character to the feel. (0:04)

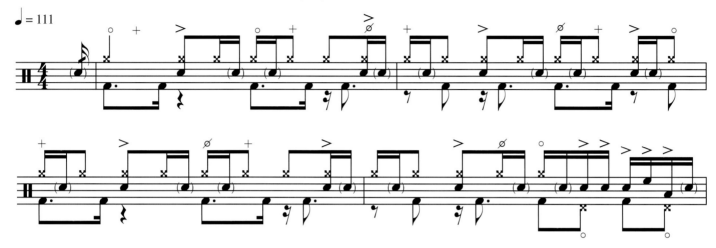

He accompanies the vocal melody of the chorus with a straightforward 8th-note groove. The hi-hat swells at the end of the section adding tension without the use of extra notes. (0:46)

"Goodbye Hooray," *I'm with You*

The jagged rhythms on the intro of "Goodbye Hooray" spawn a satisfyingly syncopated drum groove. Chad's offbeat kick and snare accents pop nicely under the solid quarter-note feel on the open hi-hat. (0:01)

He straightens out the bass drum pattern and switches to the ride cymbal in the chorus. (0:36)

The Music

Chad opens up in the outro with fast four-stroke ruffs and singles. (3:26)

"Purple Stain," *Californication*

At the beginning of "Purple Stain," a spacious groove leaves plenty of room for the ultra-funky bass and rhythm guitar to shine. (0:02)

The Music

Chad spices things up in the pre-chorus by adding ghost notes and interacting with the guitar riff with the bass drum. (0:55)

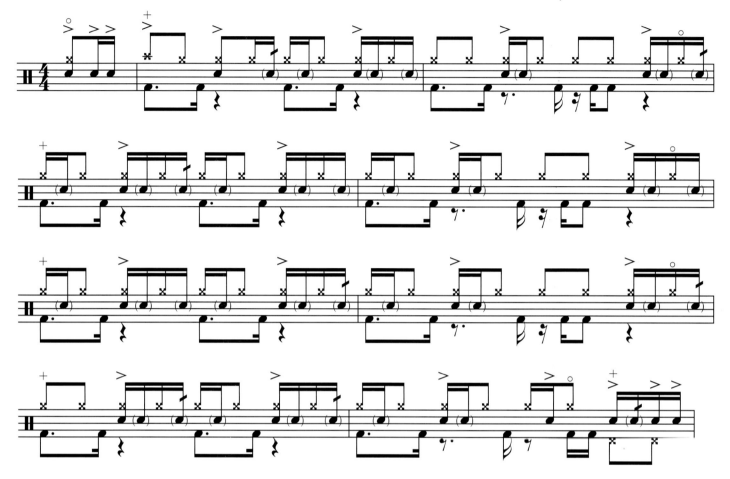

As the outro builds, Smith escalates the activity with 32nd-note doubles between the ride and snare. When the band hits the peak, he lets it rip with blazing-fast extended single-stroke rolls from the snare to the cymbals. (2:43)

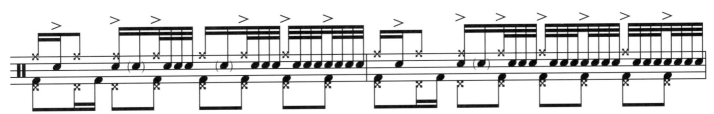

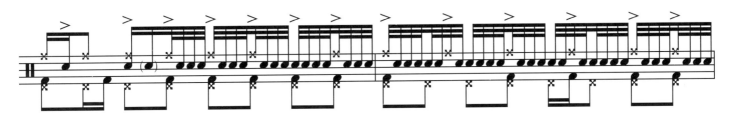

The Music

"Dark Necessities," *The Getaway*

Chad's groove on "Dark Necessities" has a backbeat only on beat 2, giving it a unique feel. He takes a minimalistic approach in the verse, leaving the fills for other elements in the production. The hi-hat carries the time with a 16th-note feel. (0:42)

In the chorus, the hi-hat switches to 8th notes at the end of the measure and leaves space for the tambourine to fill in the 16ths. Chad brings the verse back in with a smooth fill from the snare to the toms. (1:33)

In the bridge, Chad brings in the second backbeat on beat 4 to anchor the band as the different instruments spiral off to play independently. His right foot taps out some quick 16th-note figures that lead into the second measure of the phrase. He plays a decisive fill to bring the band in at the end of the section. (2:46)

The guitar solo outro showcases more of Chad's wicked right-foot control. His kick plays busy 16th-note rhythms that both push the guitar lead and accentuate the bass part. (4:02)

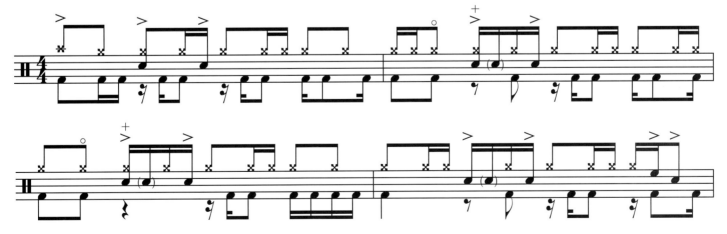

The Music

"Big Foot," *Chickenfoot*

"Big Foot" is a no-nonsense rocker from the supergroup Chickenfoot. Smith plays a driving 8th-note beat on the intro and subtly opens the hi-hat on the downbeats to give the groove forward momentum. (0:00)

♩ = 97

Throughout the song, Chad builds a theme by emphasizing the "and" of count one, as it works with the vocal lines' contour. He creatively phrases over the bar going into the chorus on the snare. (0:38)

Chad outlines the instrumental interlude with a syncopated groove on the snare and kick. As he builds through the section, the over-the-bar fills set up the band's rhythmic figures. (1:58)

The Music

"Need Strange," *Meet the Meatbats*

Chad Smith's Bombastic Meatbats is an instrumental funk/rock/fusion group formed in 2007. Smith gets to let his chops out of the bag in this setting, and the song "Need Strange" is a great vehicle for his style. Chad stretches out with some solo phrases over the groovy keyboard vamp on the intro. (0:00)

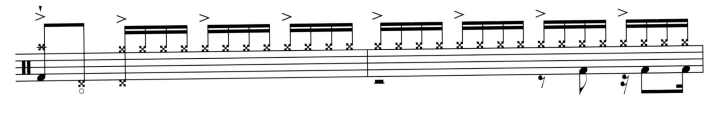

On the B section, Chad plays a James Brown-style beat. The snare lands on the downbeat, the "and" of 2, and on beat 4. (1:09)

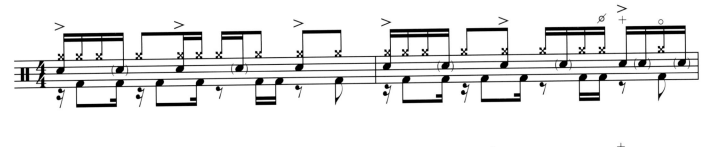

The Music

The drums get the spotlight in the middle of the song to set up the bridge. Smith effortlessly fires accents around the kit while the left foot holds it all together with steady 8th notes. (2:24)

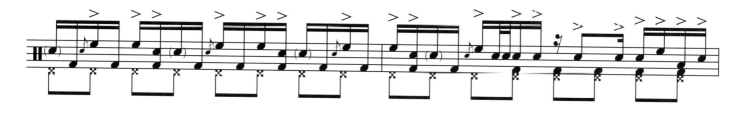

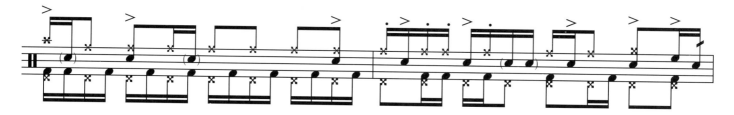

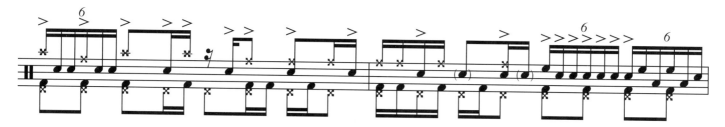

Tony Woolliscroft

Tony Woolliscroft

Tony Woolliscroft

Tony Woolliscroft